# Japanese Verbs at a Glance

D1334264

# JAPANESE VERBS AT A GLANCE

**Naoko Chino**

**Translated by Tom Gally**

KODANSHA INTERNATIONAL
Tokyo • New York • London

Distributed in the United States by Kodansha America, Inc., 114 Fifth Avenue, New York, N.Y. 10011, and in the United Kingdom and continental Europe by Kodansha Europe Ltd., 95 Aldwych, London WC2B 4JF. Published by Kodansha International Ltd., 17-14 Otowa 1-chome, Bunkyo-ku, Tokyo 112, and Kodansha America, Inc.

# CONTENTS

# About This Book

This book provides useful information about verbs for beginning and intermediate students of Japanese. It's a handy reference to turn to when you have questions about Japanese verbs and how to use them.

Charts and tables make the key points understandable at a glance, and the many example sentences show how to use verbs correctly in context. This book does not attempt a complete exposition of Japanese grammar. Instead, it provides a wealth of practical information in one specific area for people who need to speak or write Japanese.

The book is organized according to how verbs are used. If you want to know how to ask a person to do something, for example, just check the Index for "asking favors and making requests" and go to that page.

Special sections are devoted to areas of Japanese verbs that often cause difficulty for students, including polite forms, causatives, passives, and transitive/intransitive pairs. Each of these areas is covered clearly and in detail with charts, explanations, and example sentences.

Finally, the appendix lists the conjugations of verbs that are most often encountered by beginning and intermediate students. If you are unsure how to conjugate a verb correctly, a quick trip to the back of the book will provide the answer.

# まえがき

　外国人と日本語の勉強をしていて気づく事の一つに、中級程度の力のある人でも動詞の変化などを正しく覚えていない事があります。この本は初級から中級の学習者が動詞について疑問をもった時、また使い方が分からない時に役に立つ事を目的にしています。従って初級から中級のレベルにかけての必要な動詞の知識はだいたい取り上げてあります。しかしこの本は従来のような文法書として書いたものではありませんので、説明はできるだけ短くし、その代わりチャートを使って見てすぐ理解でき、応用できるよう工夫してあります。そして各項目には例文がつけてありますので、正しい使い方を学ぶ事ができるとともに、作文の練習にも役立ちます。

　この本の特徴は、各項目を機能によって分けたことです。例えば、読者が人にものを頼む時どういう動詞を使うか知りたければ、目次から（あるいは索引から）「依頼するときの言い方」を見ていただくと分かるようになっています。

　動詞の中で難しいと考えられている、受け身、使役、敬語、自動詞、他動詞なども、項目別に、チャートや表そして例文等で分かりやすく説明してあります。動詞の活用に関しては中級までによく使う動詞を選び、リストにして付録の頁に載せてあります。動詞の活用が分からない時には、その部分を参照してください。

　この本は日本語を勉強なさる外国人の方々ばかりでなく、新しく日本語を教え始めた教師の方々が学生を指導なさる時にお使いいただけたらと思います。終りにこの本の英訳をして下さったトム・ガリーさん、編集を担当して下さったマイケル・ブレーズさんと鈴木重好さんに心から感謝を申し上げます。

# About Japanese Verbs

The meanings and functions of Japanese verbs vary according to the suffixes that are attached to the verb stem. These verb conjugation patterns, which determine the forms of the suffixes, fall into three main categories:

1 When the verb stem ends in a consonant
2 When the verb stem ends in a vowel
3 When the verb is irregular

In some languages, such as French or English, the rules for conjugating verbs are quite complex, but in Japanese they are relatively simple, partly because the conjugation patterns are not affected by gender, person, or number. Even tense conjugations are quite regular. Whereas in English many common verbs (such as *go*) have irregular forms for the past tense (*went*) and past participle (*gone*), Japanese rules for the formal and informal past tense apply equally to all verbs with only a handful of exceptions.

One irregular form in Japanese is the copula *da* だ, which corresponds roughly to "be" verbs in English. Its basic forms are the formal present *desu* です, the informal past *datta* だった, and the formal past *deshita* でした.

As in English, there are both transitive and intransitive verbs. But not all verbs are paired in this way, and Japanese transitivity is quite different from that in English. This feature of Japanese is explained in the section on transitive and intransitive verbs (p. 74).

Perhaps the most complicated area of Japanese verbs is *keigo* 敬語, or polite language. In Japanese, the level of politeness varies depending on the relative age and social position of the speaker and hearer. While the full ins-and-outs of Japanese polite language are quite complex, there is an easy solution for students who are afraid that an inappropriate form may sound rude: use the verb's formal (*-masu* ーます) form. It will be appropriate in almost any situation. Later, as your understanding of polite language deepens, you'll be able to branch out into more sophisticated structures that will help you better understand and communicate with Japanese people.

# Abbreviations

| Abbreviation | Meaning | Examples |
|---|---|---|
| ① | Group 1 verbs (consonant-stem verbs) | *nomu* 飲む *tatsu* 立つ |
| ② | Group 2 verbs (vowel-stem verbs) | *taberu* 食べる *miru* 見る |
| ③ | Group 3 verbs (irregular verbs) | *kuru* 来る *suru* する |
| [ ] | Shows the plain form of verbs used in illustrative examples. | [*nomu* 飲む] |
| */-masu/* ／ーます／ | Form of verbs after the final *-masu* ーます has been removed; removal of *-masu* is often indicated thus: /~~masu~~/ ／~~ます~~／; the result might be called the "/-*masu*/ stem"; to be distinguished from the *-masu* form itself, which has *-masu* appended (e.g., *tabemasu* 食べます) | *nomi*/~~masu~~/ 飲み／~~ます~~／ *tabe*/~~masu~~/ 食べ／~~ます~~／ |

| | | |
|---|---|---|
| */-nai/ /－ない/* | Form of verbs after the final *-nai* －ない has been removed; removal of *-nai* is often indicated thus: /~~nai~~/ /~~ない~~/; the result might be called the "*/-nai/* stem"; to be distinguished from the *-nai* form itself, which has *-nai* appended (e.g., *tabenai* 食べない) | *noma/~~nai~~/* 飲ま/~~ない~~/ <br><br> *tabe/~~nai~~/* 食べ/~~ない~~/ |
| */-u/ /－う/* | Stem of the plain form of verbs after the final *-u* －う has been removed; removal of */-u/* is often indicated thus: /~~u~~/ (which can be done only in romanization) | *nom/~~u~~/* (飲む) |
| */-ru/ /－る/* | Form of verbs after the final *-ru* －る has been removed; removal of *-ru* is often indicated thus: /~~ru~~/ /~~る~~/ | *tabe/~~ru~~/* 食べ/~~る~~/ |
| (neg.) | Negative form | |
| (i) | Intransitive verb | |
| (t) | Transitive verb | |

# 1

# An Outline of Japanese Verb Forms

This chapter summarizes the basic information about Japanese verbs, including the conjugation groups and the plain, *-masu*, *-te*, past tense, and negative forms.

## Conjugation Groups 動詞のグループ分け

Japanese verbs fall into three main conjugation groups according to their plain form (dictionary form). In this book, the groups are called Group 1, Group 2, and Group 3.

### Group 1: *-U* Ending

The plain form suffix of Group 1 verbs is the vowel *-u*. The conjugation pattern depends on the vowel or consonant that precedes the *-u*. In the following examples, the verbs are grouped by final syllable (left-hand column in Japanese order). In all but the first category (the *-u* category, where *-u* is preceded by a vowel), the preceding sound is a consonant (*k*, *g*, *s*, *ts*, *n*, *b*, *m*, or *r*).

| *-u* ー う | *arau* 洗う | to wash |
| | *monoiu* 物言う | to speak up |
| | *kuu* 食う | to eat (nonpolite) |
| | *hirou* 拾う | to pick up |

| -ku ー く | aruku 歩く | to walk |
| | ugoku 動く | to move |
| | kiku 聞く | to hear, to listen |
| | migaku 磨く | to polish |
| -gu ー ぐ | oyogu 泳ぐ | to swim |
| | nugu ぬぐ | to take off (clothing) |
| -su ー す | orosu 下ろす | to lower |
| | kasu 貸す | to lend |
| | kesu 消す | to extinguish |
| | hanasu 話す | to speak |
| -tsu ー つ | tatsu 立つ | to stand |
| | matsu 待つ | to wait |
| | motsu 持つ | to hold |
| -nu ー ぬ | shinu 死ぬ | to die |
| -bu ー ぶ | asobu 遊ぶ | to play |
| | tobu 飛ぶ | to fly |
| | yobu 呼ぶ | to call |
| -mu ー む | susumu 進む | to advance |
| | sumu 住む | to live |
| | nomu 飲む | to drink |
| | yomu 読む | to read |
| -ru ー る | oriru 降る | to get down |
| | owaru 終る | to end |
| | kakaru かかる | to be suspended |
| | kaburu かぶる | to put on (a hat, etc.) |
| | noru 乗る | to get on (a train, etc.) |
| | haru はる | to affix |
| | wakaru わかる | to understand |

Some Group 1 verbs end in *-iru* or *-eru*, which are the standard endings of Group 2 verbs. The following are some common *-iru* and *-eru* verbs that belong to Group 1.

| | | |
|---|---|---|
| *iru* 要る | | to be required |
| *kaeru* 帰る | | to return |
| *kiru* 切る | | to cut |
| *shiru* 知る | | to know, to find out |
| *hairu* 入る | | to enter |
| *hashiru* 走る | | to run |

## Group 2: *-Eru* and *-Iru* Endings

These verbs end in either *-eru* or *-iru*. All Group 2 verbs have the same conjugation pattern.

| *-eru* | *akeru* 開ける | to open |
|---|---|---|
| | *kakeru* かける | to suspend, to cover |
| | *taberu* 食べる | to eat |
| | *deru* 出る | to go out |
| | *neru* 寝る | to sleep |
| | *norikaeru* 乗り換える | to change (trains) |
| *-iru* | *okiru* 起きる | to get up (from bed) |
| | *oriru* 降りる | to get down |
| | *kiru* 着る | to put on (clothing) |
| | *miru* 見る | to see |

## Group 3: Irregular Verbs

This group consists of only two verbs:

| | | |
|---|---|---|
| *kuru* 来る | | to come |
| *suru* する | | to do |

## Copula

Though not strictly a verb, the copula *da* だ has several forms that correspond to verb conjugations. These forms are mentioned in the appropriate sections of this chapter.

## Terminology

Japanese textbooks and dictionaries use a variety of names for the three conjugation categories. Here are some of the more common terms.

### ■ Group 1 verbs

| | |
|---|---|
| *godan dōshi* 五段動詞 | godan verbs |
| *shiin gokan dōshi* 子音語幹動詞 | consonant-stem verbs |
| *kyōhenka dōshi* 強変化動詞 | strong verbs |
| — | *-u* verbs |

### ■ Group 2 verbs

| | |
|---|---|
| *ichidan dōshi* 一段動詞 | ichidan verbs |
| *boin gokan dōshi* 母音語幹動詞 | vowel-stem verbs |
| *jakuhenka dōshi* 弱変化動詞 | weak verbs |
| — | *-ru* verbs |

### ■ Group 3 verbs

| | |
|---|---|
| *fukisoku dōshi* 不規則動詞 | irregular verbs |
| *ka-gyō henkaku katsuyō dōshi* カ行変格活用動詞 (*ka-hen dōshi* カ変動詞) | *ka*-row irregular verb (The only example is *kuru* 来る.) |
| *sa-gyō henkaku katsuyō dōshi* サ行変格活用動詞 (*sa-hen dōshi* サ変動詞) | *sa*-row irregular verb (The only example is *suru* する.) |

# Verb Conjugations 動詞の活用

Japanese verbs conjugate according to the suffixes that attach to the verb stem. These suffixes express a wide range of meanings, including tense, negation, passive mood, and causation. Two or more suffixes may be appended to a single stem.

The following sections describe the conjugation patterns for the *-masu*, *-te*, past tense, and negative forms. The rules for attaching other suffixes are introduced later in the book.

## Plain Form or Dictionary Form 原形、辞書形 ━━━

| | |
|---|---|
| ① /-u/ | nomu 飲む |
| ② /-ru/ | taberu 食る |
| ③ kuru | 来る |
| suru | する |

The plain form is used in informal situations. It is also the form listed in dictionaries.

## The -Masu Form ます形 ━━━━━━━━

| | |
|---|---|
| ① /-~~u~~/ + imasu | |
| nom/~~u~~/ + imasu → nomimasu | 飲む → 飲みます |
| ② /-~~ru~~/ + masu | /-~~る~~/ + ます |
| tabe/~~ru~~/ + masu → tabemasu | 食べ／~~る~~/ + ます |
| | → 食べます |
| ③ kuru → kimasu | 来る → 来ます |
| suru → shimasu | する → します |

The *-masu* form is commonly used in formal situations. It is added to the plain form of the verb as follows:

① Drop the final *-u* and add *-imasu*:

    *nomu* → *nomimasu*    飲む → 飲みます
    *tatsu* → *tachimasu*    立つ → 立ちます

      Note: Final *-tsu* ーつ becomes *-chi* ーち and final *-su* ーす becomes *-shi* ーし.

② Drop the final *-ru* and add *-masu*:

    *taberu* → *tabemasu*    食べる → 食べます

③    *kuru* → *kimasu*    来る → 来ます
    *suru* → *shimasu*    する → します

Copula: The formal form of *da* だ is *desu* です.

## ■ Formal examples

① 酒を飲みます。
*Sake o nomimasu.*
I (will) drink saké.

② さしみを食べます。
*Sashimi o tabemasu.*
I (will) eat sashimi.

③ テニスをします。
*Tenisu o shimasu.*
I (will) play tennis.

Copula これは今日の新聞です。
*Kore wa kyō no shimbun desu.*
This is today's newspaper.

## ■ Informal examples

① 酒を飲む。
*Sake o nomu.*
I (will) drink saké.

② さしみを食べる。
*Sashimi o taberu.*
I (will) eat sashimi.

③ テニスをする。
*Tenisu o suru.*
I (will) play tennis.

Copula これは今日の新聞だ。
*Kore wa kyō no shimbun da.*
This is today's newspaper.

## The /-*Masu*/ ／－ます／ Stem

Many verb suffixes are attached to the -*masu* form of verbs after the *masu* ます has been removed, leaving what might be called the /-*masu*/ stem. In this book the removal of *masu* is indicated by placing it within slashes and striking through it (/~~masu~~/). Examples follow for the three verb groups, the plain form followed by the -*masu* form with the -*masu* struck through, leaving the /-*masu*/ stem.

| | |
|---|---|
| ① *nomu* → *nomi*/~~masu~~/ | 飲む → 飲み／~~ます~~／ |
|     *tatsu* → *tachi*/~~masu~~/ | 立つ → 立ち／~~ます~~／ |
| ② *taberu* → *tabe*/~~masu~~/ | 食べる → 食べ／~~ます~~／ |
| ③ *kuru* → *ki*/~~masu~~/ | 来る → 来／~~ます~~／ |
|     *suru* → *shi*/~~masu~~/ | する → し／~~ます~~／ |

## The -*Te* Form て形

| | |
|---|---|
| ① (See chart below.) | |
| ② /-~~ru~~/ + *te* | ／－~~る~~／ + て |

|   |   |   |
|---|---|---|
| | *tabe/ru̶/* + *te* → *tabete* | 食べ／呑／＋て → 食べて |
| ③ | *kuru* → *kite* | 来る → 来て |
| | *suru* → *shite* | する → して |

The *-te* form is used to link clauses together and to show the order of actions, in addition to many other functions. It is formed as shown below.

The *-te* form of Group 1 verbs varies depending on the sound that precedes the final *-u* in the plain form.

| Rule | Example | Example |
|------|---------|---------|
| ① | | |
| *-au = a/u̶/* + *tte* | *arau* → *aratte* | 洗う → 洗って |
| *-iu = i/u̶/* + *tte* | *monoiu* → *monoitte* | 物言う → 物言って |
| *-uu = u/u̶/* + *tte* | *kuu* → *kutte* | 食う → 食って |
| *-ou = o/u̶/* + *tte* | *hirou* → *hirotte* | 拾う → 拾って |
| *-ku = /ku̶/* + *ite* | *kiku* → *kiite* | 聞く → 聞いて |
| | Note (irregular form): *iku* → *itte* | 行く → 行って |
| *-gu = /gu̶/* + *ide* | *oyogu* → *oyoide* | 泳ぐ → 泳いで |
| *-su = /su̶/* + *shite* | *hanasu* → *hanashite* | 話す → 話して |
| *-tsu = /tsu̶/* + *tte* | *matsu* → *matte* | 待つ → 待って |
| *-nu = /nu̶/* + *nde* | *shinu* → *shinde* | 死ぬ → 死んで |
| *-bu = /bu̶/* + *nde* | *asobu* → *asonde* | 遊ぶ → 遊んで |
| *-mu = /mu̶/* + *nde* | *yomu* → *yonde* | 読む → 読んで |
| *-ru = /ru̶/* + *tte* | *kaeru* → *kaette* | 帰る → 帰って |
| | *hashiru* → *hashitte* | 走る → 走って |
| | *noru* → *notte* | 乗る → 乗って |

| ② | | |
|---|---|---|
| -eru = e/r̶u̶/ + te | teberu → tabete | 食べる → 食べて |
| -iru = i/r̶u̶/ + te | miru → mite | 見る → 見て |
| ③ | | |
| | kuru → kite | 来る → 来て |
| | suru → shite | する → して |

Copula: The -te
form of da だ
is de で.

---

# Tense テンス

## Present and Future 現在形と未来形 ——————

The present and future tenses are expressed by the -masu
form in formal use and by the plain form in informal use.

### ■ Formal present-tense examples

原：いつも何時に起きますか。
広瀬：7時に起きます。
*Hara: Itsumo nanji ni okimasu ka.*
*Hirose: Shichiji ni okimasu.*
Hara: What time do you get up every day?
Hirose: I get up at seven o'clock.

### ■ Informal present-tense examples

原：いつも何時に起きる？
広瀬：7時に起きる。
*Hara: Itsumo nanji ni okiru?*
*Hirose: Shichiji ni okiru.*
Hara: When do you get out of bed every day?
Hirose: I'm up at seven.

## ■Formal future-tense examples

田中：明日は何時に家を出ますか。
山口：8時に出ます。
*Tanaka: Ashita wa nanji ni ie o demasu ka?*
*Yamaguchi: Hachi-ji ni demasu.*
Tanaka: What time will you leave home tomorrow?
Yamaguchi: I'll leave at 8 o'clock.

## ■Informal future-tense examples

田中：明日は何時に家を出る？
山口：8時に出るよ。
*Tanaka: Ashita wa nanji ni ie o deru?*
*Yamaguchi: Hachi-ji ni deru yo.*
Tanaka: When are you going to leave home tomorrow?
Yamaguchi: At 8 o'clock.

## Past 過去形 ────────────

---

Formal

    *-masu → -mashita*　　　　　ます → ました
      *nomi/~~masu~~/ → nomimashita*　飲み／~~ます~~／ →
                           飲みました

Informal

① ② *-te → -ta*　　　　　　　て → た
     *tabe/~~te~~/ → tabeta*　　食べ／~~て~~／ → 食べた
    *-de → -da*　　　　　　で → だ
     *non/~~de~~/ → nonda*　　飲ん／~~で~~／ → 飲んだ
③　*kuru → kita*　　　　来る → 来た
   *suru → shita*　　　　　する → した

Copula: *da* だ has the formal past tense *deshita* でした
and the informal past tense *datta* だった.

---

The formal past tense of Groups 1 and 2 verbs is formed from the *-masu* form by replacing the final *-masu* ーます with *-mashita* ーました.

*nomimasu* → *nomimashita*　飲みます → 飲みました
　　　　　　　　　　　　　　　[飲む *nomu*]

The informal past tense verbs are formed by replacing the final *-e* of the *-te* or *-de* form with *-a*:

*nonde* →*nonda*　　　　　飲んで → 飲んだ
*mite* → *mita*　　　　　　見て → 見た [見る *miru*]

The irregular Group 3 verbs have the following formal past tense forms:

*kuru* → *kimashita*　　　来る → 来ました
*suru* → *shimashita*　　　する → しました

The informal past forms for Group 3 are:

*kuru* → *kita*　　　　　　来る → 来た
*suru* → *shita*　　　　　　する → した

## ■ Formal examples

田中：昨日は山田さんに会いましたよ。 [会う *au*]
山口：山田さんに。元気でしたか。 [だ *da*]
*Tanaka: Kinō wa Yamada-san ni aimashita yo.*
*Yamaguchi: Yamada-san ni? Genki deshita ka?*
Tanaka (male): I met Ms. Yamada yesterday.
Yamaguchi (male): Ms. Yamada? How was she?

## ■ Informal examples

田中：昨日は山田さんに会ったよ。
山口：山田さんに。元気だったか。
*Tanaka: Kinō wa Yamada-san ni atta yo.*
*Yamaguchi: Yamada-san ni? Genki datta ka?*
Tanaka (male): I saw Ms. Yamada yesterday.
Yamaguchi (male): Ms. Yamada? How is she doing?

## Negatives　否定形

The negative form is often called the "*-nai* form" because the informal present tense ends in *-nai* ーない.

## ■Present Negative 現在否定形

| | | |
|---|---|---|
| **Formal** | | |
| *-masu* → *-masen* | | ます → ません |
| *nomimasu* → *nomimasen* | | 飲みます → 飲みません |
| **Informal** | | |
| ① /-u̶/ + *-anai* | | |
| *ik/u̶/anai* | | 行く → 行かない |
| ② /-r̶u̶/ + *-nai* | | /-r̶u̶/ + ない |
| *tabe/r̶u̶/nai* | | 食べ／る̶／ない |
| ③ *kuru* → *konai* | | 来る → 来ない |
| *suru* → *shinai* | | する → しない |

The formal present negative of all verbs is formed from the *-masu* form by replacing the final *-masu* ーます with *-masen* ーません.

 *ikimasu* → *ikimasen*　行きます → 行きません [行く *iku*]

The informal present negative of Group 1, 2, and 3 verbs is formed as follows:

① If the final *-u* in the plain form is preceded by a consonant, change the *-u* to *-anai*:

 *iku* → *ikanai*　　行く → 行かない
 *tatsu* →*tatanai*　立つ → 立たない
　　Note: Final *-tsu* ーつ becomes *-tanai* ーたない.

If the final *-u* is preceded by a vowel, change the *-u* to *-wanai*. Note that *-w-* is inserted to separate the vowels.

 *au* → *awanai*　　会う → 会わない

② Drop the final *-ru* ーる and add *-nai* ーない.

 *taberu* → *tabenai*　食べる → 食べない

③　 *kuru* → *konai*　来る → 来ない
　　 *suru* → *shinai*　する → しない

The negative form of the copula *da* だ is *de wa nai* ではない. In conversation, this form is often contracted to *ja nai* じゃない.

● Formal examples

田中：テニスをしますか。 [する]
山口：私はテニスはしません。
*Tanaka: Tenisu o shimasu ka?*
*Yamaguchi: Watashi wa tenisu wa shimasen.*
Tanaka: Do you play tennis?
Yamaguchi: No, I don't play tennis.

● Informal examples

田中：テニスをする？
山口：しない。
*Tanaka: Tenisu o suru?*
*Yamaguchi: Shinai.*
Tanaka: You play tennis?
Yamaguchi: No, I don't.

● The */-Nai/* ／－ない／ Stem

Some verb suffixes are attached to the informal present negative form of verbs after the *-nai* －ない suffix has been removed. This form is called the */-nai/* stem and is abbreviated /-~~nai~~/ ／－~~ない~~／ in charts. Here are examples of */-nai/* stems:

| | |
|---|---|
| ① *nomu → noma-* | 飲む → 飲まー |
| *tatsu → tata-* | 立つ → 立たー |
| ② *taberu → tabe-* | 食べる → 食べー |
| ③ *kuru → ko-* | 来る → 来ー |
| *suru → shi-* | する → しー |

■ **Past Negative** 過去形

| Formal |
|---|
| *-masen → -masen deshita*　　ません → ませんでした |
| *ikimasen → ikimasen deshita*　行きません → |
| 行きませんでした |

> *mimasen* → *mimasen deshita*　見ません →
> 　　　　　　　　　　　　　　　　見ませんでした
>
> **Informal**
> 　*nai* → *-nakatta*　　　　　　ない → なかった
> 　*ikanai* → *ikanakatta*　　　行かない →
> 　　　　　　　　　　　　　　　　行かなかった
> 　*minai* → *minakatta*　　　　見ない → 見なかった

The formal past negative of all verbs is formed by adding *deshita* でした after the formal present negative (*-masen* ーません) form:

　*ikimasen* → *ikimasen deshita*　行きません → 行きま
　　　　　　　　　　　　　　　　　せんでした [行く *iku*]

The informal past negative is formed by changing the final *-nai* ーない of the informal negative to *-nakatta* ーなかった.

● Formal examples
　山田：田中さんは午後、会社にいましたか。 [いる *iru*]
　佐藤：いいえ、いませんでした。
　*Yamada: Tanaka-san wa gogo, kaisha ni imashita ka?*
　*Satō: Īe, imasen deshita.*
　Yamada: Was Mr. Tanaka at the company during the afternoon?
　Satō: No, he wasn't.

● Informal examples
　山田：田中さんは午後、会社にいた？
　佐藤：いや、いなかった。
　*Yamada: Tanaka-san wa gogo, kaisha ni ita?*
　*Satō: Iya, inakatta.*
　Yamada: Was Tanaka in the office this afternoon?
　Satō: No, he wasn't.

# 2

# How Verbs Are Used

## Formal Forms ていねいな表現

In situations requiring politeness or a degree of formality, the *-masu* form (see Chapter 1) is used. Forms expressing more pronounced formality are discussed below under the heading "Polite Forms 敬語."

今日は銀座へ行きます。
*Kyō wa Ginza e ikimasu.*
I will go to Ginza today.

In informal settings among friends and family, the plain form is used.

今日は銀座へ行くよ。 [spoken by man]
*Kyō wa Ginza e iku yo.*
I'm going to Ginza today.

今日は銀座へ行くわ。 [spoken by woman]
*Kyō wa Ginza e iku wa.*
I'll be off to Ginza today.

# Continuing Actions 動作の継続を表す言い方

---

Formal

*-te + imasu* ーて＋います

① *kiku* → *kiite imasu*　　　聞く → 聞いています

② *taberu* → *tabete imasu*　　食べる → 食べています

③ *kuru* → *kite imasu*　　　来る → 来ています

　*suru* → *shite imasu*　　　する → しています

Informal

*-te + iru* ーて＋いる

① *kiku* → *kiite iru*　　　　聞く → 聞いている

② *taberu* → *tabete iru*　　　食べる → 食べている

③ *kuru* → *kite iru*　　　　来る → 来ている

　*suru* → *shite iru*　　　　する → している

Continuing actions are expressed by the *-te* form followed by *imasu* います (formal) or *iru* いる (informal).

## Present Progressive 動作が現在続いている場合 ——

The *-te* form followed by *imasu* います or *iru* いる can be used to describe actions that are taking place in the present. This form is often translated with the *-ing* form of English verbs.

田中：鈴木さん、いますか。
佐藤：はい、でも今、電話をしています。 [する *suru*]
*Tanaka: Suzuki-san, imasu ka?*
*Satō: Hai, demo ima, denwa o shite imasu.*
Tanaka: Is Ms. Suzuki here?
Satō: Yes, but she's making a telephone call now.

In speech, the verb ending may be contracted to *-te 'masu* ーてます or, as in the following example, *-te 'ru* ーてる.

太郎：花子はどこ？

二郎：部屋でテレビ見てる。 [= 見ている *mite iru*, from
　　見る *miru*]

*Tarō: Hanako wa doko?*
*Jirō: Heya de terebi mite 'ru.*
Tarō: Where's Hanako?
Jirō: She's watching TV in her room.

## Habitual Actions 動作が習慣的に繰り返して 行なわれる場合 ━━━━━━━━

The *-te* form plus *imasu* います or *iru* いる can also describe constant states or repeated actions.

佐藤さんは千代田区に住んでいます。 [住む *sumu*]
*Satō-san wa Chiyoda-ku ni sunde imasu.*
Mr. Satō lives in Chiyoda Ward.

伊藤さんは貿易会社で働いている。 [働く *hataraku*]
*Itō-san wa bōeki-gaisha de hataraite iru.*
Ms. Itō works at a trading company.

## Conditions 状態を表す場合 ━━━━━━━━━━━━━

This form can also describe a condition or situation.

多田：東京の地下鉄はいつも混んでいますね。[混む *komu*]
森：本当ですね。
*Tada: Tōkyō no chikatetsu wa itsumo konde imasu ne.*
*Mori: Hontō desu ne.*
Tada: Tokyo subways are always crowded.
Mori: That's really true.

佐藤さんは、時々眼鏡をかけています。
*Satō-san wa, toki-doki megane o kakete imasu.*
Mr. Satō sometimes wears glasses.

後藤：山田さんの部屋の電気がついていますね。[つく
　　*tsuku*]
山口：そうですね。部屋にいるかもしれませんね。
*Gotō: Yamada-san no heya no denki ga tsuite imasu ne.*
*Yamaguchi: Sō desu ne. Heya ni iru kamo shiremasen ne.*
Gotō: The light's on in Mrs. Yamada's room.
Yamaguchi: So it is. Maybe she's in the room.

# Asking Favors and Making Requests 相手に何かを頼む言い方

There are many ways to ask favors and make requests in Japanese depending on the relationship between the speaker and hearer. The following sections describe some of the most common patterns.

## Polite Requests

| | |
|---|---|
| (1) *-te + itadakemasen ka*<br>*mite itadakemasen ka?* | ーて＋いただけませんか<br>見ていただけませんか。[見る *miru*] |
| (2) *-te + kudasaimasen ka*<br>*shite kudasaimasen ka?* | ーて＋くださいませんか<br>してくださいませんか。[する *suru*] |
| (3) *-nai + de itadakemasen ka*<br>*minai de itadakemasen ka?* | ーない＋でいただけませんか<br>見ないでいただけませんか。[見る *miru*] |
| (4) *-nai + de kudasaimasen ka*<br>*shinai de kudasaimasen ka?* | ーない＋でくださいませんか<br>しないでくださいませんか。[する *suru*] |

As in English, polite requests in Japanese often take the form of a question. The first two of the patterns shown here use the *-te* form, while the second pair use the plain negative (*-nai*) form. The latter has a softening effect.

■ **(1) *-te + itadakemasen ka*　ーて＋いただけませんか**
店員：すみませんが、こちらにご住所を書いていただけませんか。[書く *kaku*]
お客：いいですよ。

*Ten'in: Sumimasen ga, kochira ni go-jūsho o kaite itadake-masen ka?*

*O-kyaku: Ii desu yo.*

Store clerk: Excuse me, but would you please write your address here?

Customer: Okay.

■ **(2) -te + kudasaimasen ka** ーて + くださいませんか

明日電話をしてくださいませんか。

*Myōnichi denwa o shite kudasaimasen ka?*

Could you please call tomorrow?

■ **(3) -nai + de itadakemasen ka** ーない + でいただけませんか

すみません、ここでタバコを吸わないでいただけませんか。[吸う *suu*]

*Sumimasen, koko de tabako o suwanai de itadakemasen ka?*

Excuse me, would you please not smoke here?

■ **(4) -nai + de kudasaimasen ka** ーない + でくださいませんか

ここにごみを捨てないでくださいませんか。[捨てる *suteru*]

*Koko ni gomi o sutenai de kudasaimasen ka?*

Would you please refrain from throwing away trash here?

## Placing Orders, Requesting Delivery and Repairs, etc.
注文や配達、修理などを頼む時の言い方 ━━━━━

| | |
|---|---|
| (1) *-te + hoshii n' desu (ga)* | ーて+ほしいんです（が） |
| *naoshite hoshii n' desu ga.* | 直してほしいんですが。 [直す *naosu*] |
| (2) *-te + moraitai n' desu (ga)* | ーて+もらいたいんです（が） |
| *todokete moraitai n' desu ga.* | 届けてもらいたいんです が。[届ける *todokeru*] |

These two largely interchangable forms can be used when

making purchases or asking to have something delivered or repaired.

■ **(1)** *-te + hoshii n' desu (ga)*  ーて + ほしいんです（が）

お客：時計を直してほしいんですが。
店員：ちょっと見せてください。

*O-kyaku: Tokei o naoshite hoshii n' desu ga.*
*Ten'in: Chotto misete kudasai.*

Customer: I'd like to have a watch repaired.
Store clerk: Let me take a look at it.

■ **(2)** *-te + moraitai n' desu (ga)*  ーて + もらいたいんです（が）

The verb *moraitai* もらいたい is the *-tai* form of *morau* もらう.

お客：すしを五人前届けてもらいたいんですが。
すし屋：かしこまりました。お名前とご住所をどうぞ。

*O-kyaku: Sushi o gonin-mae todokete moraitai n' desu ga.*
*Sushi-ya: Kashikomarimashita. O-namae to go-jūsho o dōzo.*

Customer: I'd like to have five servings of sushi delivered.
Sushi seller: Very well. Your name and address, please.

---

## Commands and Prohibitions 命令と禁止を表す言い方

---

### Commands 命令 ━━━━━━━━━━━━

| Polite | |
|---|---|
| *-te + kudasaimasen ka* | ーて + くださいませんか |
| *sutte kudasaimasen ka* | 吸ってくださいませんか [吸う *suu*] |
| *-nai + de kudasaimasen ka* (neg.) | ーない + でくださいませんか |

| | |
|---|---|
| *suwanaide kudasai-masen ka* | 吸わないでくださいませんか |

Note: The latter is slightly more polite.

## Formal

| | |
|---|---|
| *-te + kudasai* | ー て ＋ ください |
| *sutte kudasai* | 吸ってください |
| *-nai + de kudasai* (neg.) | ー ない ＋ でください |
| *suwanaide kudasai* | 吸わないでください |
| *-mashō* | ー ましょう |
| *suimashō* | 吸いましょう |

## Informal

| | |
|---|---|
| *-te* | ー て |
| *tabete* | 食べて [食べる *taberu*] |
| *-nai de* (neg.) | ー ないで |
| *tabenai de* | 食べないで |
| *-te + chōdai* | ー て ＋ ちょうだい |
| *tabete chōdai* | 食べてちょうだい |
| */~~masu~~/ + nasai* | ／ ー ~~ます~~ ／ ＋ なさい |
| *tabe/~~masu~~/nasai* | 食べ／~~ます~~／なさい |
| *-te + kure* | ー てくれ |
| *tabete kure* | 食べてくれ |
| *-nai + de kure* (neg.) | ー ないでくれ |
| *tabenai de kure* | 食べないでくれ |
| */~~masu~~/ + na* | ／~~ます~~／ ＋ な |
| *tabe/~~masu~~/na* | 食べ／~~ます~~／な |

## Blunt

| | |
|---|---|
| ① */~~ru~~/ + e* | |
| *kik/~~u~~/e* | 聞く → 聞け |

② /-~~ru~~/ + ro          /一~~る~~/ + ろ

  tabe/~~ru~~/ro          食べ/~~る~~/ろ

③ kuru → koi          来る → 来い

  suru → shiro or seyo       する → しろ or せよ

When giving a command or telling someone not to do something, it's especially important to choose the right level of politeness and formality.

## ■ Polite

For polite commands, use the *-te* form followed by *kudasaimasen ka* くださいませんか:

> タバコは外で吸ってくださいませんか。[吸う *suu*]
> *Tabako wa soto de sutte kudasaimasen ka.*
> Would you please be so kind as to smoke outside?

To make a negative command—that is, to tell someone not to do something—use the plain negative (*-nai*) form of the verb followed by *de kudasaimasen ka* でくださいませんか. The negative form is somewhat more polite than the positive form.

> ここでタバコを吸わないでくださいませんか。
> *Koko de tabako o suwanai de kudasaimasen ka.*
> Would you be so kind as not to smoke here?

## ■ Formal

Formal commands can be given with the *-te* form followed by *kudasai* ください:

> タバコは外で吸ってください。
> *Tabako wa soto de sutte kudasai.*
> Please smoke outside.

Teachers use this pattern to give directions to students.

> 教師：この宿題を明日までにしてください。[する *suru*]
> 学生：はい、わかりました。
> *Kyōshi: Kono shukudai o ashita made ni shite kudasai.*

*Gakusei: Hai, wakarimashita.*
Teacher: Please do this homework by tomorrow.
Student: Okay, I will.

The negative command is made with the plain negative (*-nai*) form followed by *de kudasai* でください.

ここでタバコを吸わないでください。
*Koko de tabako o suwanai de kudasai.*
Please do not smoke here.

An indirect way of telling people what to do is to use the formal volitional form. Add *-mashō* —ましょう to the */-masu/* stem.

タバコは外で吸いましょう。
*Tabako wa soto de suimashō.*
Let's have people smoke outside.

## ■ Informal

The *-te* form can be used by itself to make informal commands among family or close friends.

食べて。 [食べる *taberu*]
*Tabete.*
Eat!

広田：その写真見せて。 [見せる *miseru*]
山口：だめよ。
*Hirota: Sono shashin misete.*
*Yamaguchi: Dame yo.*
Hirota: Hey, show me the picture.
Yamaguchi: No way!

The negative version of this form is the plain negative (*-nai*) form followed by *-de* —で.

それは食べないで。 [食べる *taberu*]
*Sore wa tabenai de.*
Don't eat that.

The *-te* form followed by *chōdai* ちょうだい is slightly more formal than the *-te* form by itself. As in the following example, adults often use *-te + chōdai* ー て + ちょうだい when speaking to children or informally to other people of an equal or lower status. This pattern is more often heard in women's speech than men's.

母親：ちょっと手伝ってちょうだい。 [手伝う *tetsudau*]
子供：これから遊びに行くからあとでね。
*Hahaoya: Chotto tetsudatte chōdai.*
*Kodomo: Kore kara asobi ni iku kara ato de ne.*
Mother: Could you help me a bit?
Child: I'm going out to play now. I'll do it later.

Another type of informal command is formed by adding *-nasai* ーなさい after the */-masu/* stem. This form is often used by mothers to their children or by teachers to their students.

早く行きなさい。 [行く *iku*]
*Hayaku ikinasai.*
Hurry up.

The word *kure* くれ can be used after the *-te* form as a blunt command in informal situations. It is characteristic of men's speech.

やめてくれ。 [やめる *yameru*]
*Yamete kure.*
Stop it.

In the negative, *kure* くれ follows the plain negative (*-nai*) plus *de* で. This pattern is characteristic of men's speech.

タバコは中で吸わないでくれ。
*Tabako wa naka de suwanai de kure.*
Don't smoke inside.

The particle *na* な is added after the *-masu* form to make an informal command. Note that, despite its resemblance to the negative *-nai* ーない suffix, this *na* な is affirmative. It is characteristic of men's speech.

早く行きな。 [行く *iku*]
*Hayaku ikina.*
Hurry up.

## ■Blunt

The following pattern, sometimes called the brusque imperative, is used for very blunt commands. It is characteristic of men's speech.

---

① Replace the final *-u* with *-e*:

    *iku* → *ike*              行く → 行け

    *tatsu* → *tate*         立つ → 立て

② Replace the final *-ru* with *-ro*:

    *taberu* → *tabero*     食べる → 食べろ

③ *kuru* → *koi*            来る → 来い

  *suru* → *shiro* or *seyo*     する → しろ or せよ

---

● Examples

すぐ来い。[来る *kuru*]
*Sugu koi.*
Come quick.

早くしろ。[する *suru*]
*Hayaku shiro.*
Do it fast.

As shown by the following examples, this blunt imperative is sometimes used rhetorically.

雨よ、降れ。[降る *furu*]
*Ame yo, fure.*
Fall, O rain!

明日天気になれ。[なる *naru*]
*Ashita tenki ni nare.*
O, let it be a fine day tomorrow.

## Prohibitions 禁止 ▬▬▬▬▬▬▬▬▬

---

Formal

  *-te* + *wa dame desu*        ーて + はだめです

| | |
|---|---|
| *sutte wa dame desu* | 吸ってはだめです |
| *-te + wa ikemasen* | ーて＋はいけません |
| *sutte wa ikemasen* | 吸ってはいけません |

Informal

| | |
|---|---|
| *-te + wa dame da* | ーて＋はだめだ |
| *sutte wa dame da* | 吸ってはだめだ |
| *-te + wa ikenai* | ーて＋はいけない |
| *sutte wa ikenai* | 吸ってはいけない |
| plain form + *bekarazu* | 原形＋べからず |
| *suu bekarazu* | 吸うべからず |
| plain form + *na* | 原形＋な |
| *suu na* | 吸うな |

The following are several strategies for forbidding somebody from doing something.

■ **Formal**

The word *dame* だめ means that something is no good,
wrong, or objectionable, so the *-te* form followed by *wa
dame desu* はだめです means that one cannot or should not
do something.

波が高いから、泳いではだめです。 [泳ぐ *oyogu*]
*Nami ga takai kara, oyoide wa dame desu.*
The waves are high, so you shouldn't go swimming.

Another way to say the same thing is with *ikemasen* いけ
ません, the negative potential form of *iku* 行く:

お酒を飲んではいけません。 [飲む *nomu*]
*O-sake o nonde wa ikemasen.*
You shouldn't drink alcohol.

■ **Informal**

In informal situations, *desu* です becomes *da* だ:

台風がきているから、海へ行ってはだめだ。 [行く *iku*]
*Taifū ga kite iru kara, umi e itte wa dame da.*
A typhoon is coming, so you can't go to the beach.

Similarly, *ikemasen* いけません becomes *ikenai* いけない:

酒を飲んではいけない。
*Sake o nonde wa ikenai.*
Don't drink alcohol.

The next pattern is used more in writing than in conversation. It often appears on warning signs. The plain form of the verb is followed by *bekarazu* べからず:

ここには入るべからず。
*Koko ni wa hairu bekarazu.*
Do not enter.

酒を飲むべからず。
*Sake o nomu bekarazu.*
Alcohol not permitted.

Another way to make a strong negative imperative in informal situations is to follow the plain form with the particle *na* な:

あの人には会うな。
*Ano hito ni wa au na.*
Don't meet that person.

Be careful not to confuse this pattern with the affirmative imperative formed with the -masu form followed by na な (see page 33).

# Polite Forms 敬語

There are two types of polite forms in Japanese: honorific and humble. The honorific form is used to show the speaker's respect toward an older person or a person in a higher social position. The humble form is used when the speaker talks about himself or herself to a superior.

## Honorifics 尊敬語

Most polite forms are derived from the plain form in a regular manner. Honorifics can be expressed in two ways, as *o* + */-masu/* + *ni naru* or by using the passive form of the verb.

### ■ *O + ... ni naru* おー ～ になる

| | |
|---|---|
| *o* + */-masu/* + *ni naru* | お + ／ー~~ます~~／ + になる |
| *o-kaki/~~masu~~/ ni naru* | お書き／~~ます~~／になる |
| | [書く *kaku*] |

In this form, the honorific prefix *o-* おー is added before the */-masu/* stem, which is then followed by the particle *ni* に and the verb *naru* なる. Since the *-masu* form of *kaku* 書く "to write" is *kakimasu* 書きます, the */-masu/* stem is *kaki* 書き and the honorific polite form is *okaki ni naru* お書きになる.

● Examples

In the following example, the student uses the honorific when speaking to her teacher.

学生：先生、今朝の新聞をお読みになりましたか。[読む *yomu*]
先生：はい、読みましたが…

*Gakusei: Sensei, kesa no shimbun o o-yomi ni nari-mashita ka?*
*Sensei: Hai, yomimashita ga...*

Student: Teacher, did you read this morning's newspaper?
Teacher: Yes, I did.

In the next example, Yamamoto uses the honorific because he is talking about the company president and his family.

山本：社長御一家が午後一時に、アメリカへおたちになるそうですね。[たつ *tatsu*]
田中：今日ですか。知りませんでした。

*Yamamoto: Shachō go-ikka ga gogo ichiji ni, Amerika e o-tachi ni naru sō desu ne.*
*Tanaka: Kyō desu ka? Shirimasen deshita.*

Yamamoto: They say that the president and his family are leaving for America at 1:00 p.m.

Tanaka: Today? I didn't know that.

## ■Using the Same Form as the Passive 受身と同じ形

| | |
|---|---|
| ① /-~~nai~~/ + reru | /ー~~ない~~/ + れる |
|    ika/~~nai~~/reru | 行か/~~ない~~/れる |
| ② /-~~nai~~/ + rareru | /ー~~ない~~/ + られる |
|    tsutome/~~nai~~/rareru | 勤め/~~ない~~/られる |
| ③ kuru → korareru | 来る → 来られる |
|    suru → sareru | する → される |

This honorific polite form is the same as the passive form, so it is created as shown by the chart above. (As mentioned on page 22, the abbreviation /-~~nai~~/ indicates that -nai is dropped; in other words, that the /-nai/ stem is used in forming the passive.)

●Examples

In the first example, Yamamoto uses the honorific when talking about the company president.

> 部長：日曜の社長の予定、わかる？
> 山本：ゴルフに行かれる予定です。[行く *iku*]
> *Buchō: Nichiyō no shachō no yotei, wakaru?*
> *Yamamoto: Gorufu ni ikareru yotei desu.*
> Division chief: Do you know the president's schedule for Sunday?
> Yamamoto: She's scheduled to go play golf.

In the next example, Yamamoto uses the honorific because he is talking to his boss.

> 山本：お宅では家具などは、どちらのデパートで買われますか。[買う *kau*]
> 課長：そうねえ、だいたい新宿のデパートだね。
> *Yamamoto: O-taku de wa kagu nado wa, dochira no depāto de kawaremasu ka?*

*Kachō: Sō nē, daitai Shinjuku no depāto da ne.*

Yamamoto: In your family, at which department store do you buy furniture and things like that?

Section chief: Usually a department store in Shinjuku, I guess.

The following example has Yamamoto using the honorific when talking about an older person.

山本：田中さんのお父さんは、成田で乗り換えられて、フランスへ向かわれるそうです。[乗り換える *norikaeru*, 向かう *mukau*]

課長：へえ、フランスまで…

*Yamamoto: Tanaka-san no otōsan wa, Narita de norikaerarete, Furansu e mukawareru sō desu.*

*Kachō: Hē, Furansu made…*

Yamamoto: I heard that Mr. Tanaka's father will change planes at Narita and head for France.

Section chief: Really, all the way to France!

The honorific is used in the next example because Yamamoto is talking to (and about) his boss.

山本：この前海水浴にいらした時は、どこに車を止められましたか。[いらっしゃる *irassharu*, 止める *tomeru*]

課長：近くに安い駐車場があってね、そこに止めた。

*Yamamoto: Kono mae kaisuiyoku ni irashita toki wa, doko ni kuruma o tomeraremashita ka?*

*Kachō: Chikaku ni yasui chūshajō ga atte ne, soko ni tometa.*

Yamamoto: Where did you park your car when you went swimming at the ocean recently?

Section chief: There's a cheap parking lot nearby. I parked it there.

The honorifics in the next dialogue are used to talk about an older person.

青木：谷さんのお母様もパーティに来られますか。[来る *kuru*]

安田：ええ、来られるだろうと思いますよ。お母様、お若い時には、よくダンスをされたそうですよ。[する *suru*]

*Aoki: Tani-san no okāsama mo pāti ni koraremasu ka?*
*Yasuda: Ē, korareru darō to omoimasu yo. Okāsama, o-wakai toki ni wa, yoku dansu o sareta sō desu yo.*

Aoki: Will Ms. Tani's mother come to the party, too?
Yasuda: Yes, I think she will. I hear that she used to dance a lot when she was young.

## Humble Forms 謙譲語

| | |
|---|---|
| *o + /-m̶a̶s̶u̶/ + suru* | お + ／―ま̶す̶／ +する |
| *o-yomi/m̶a̶s̶u̶/ shimasu* | お読み／ま̶す̶／します |
| | [読む *yomu*] |
| *o + /-m̶a̶s̶u̶/ + itashimasu* | お + ／―ま̶す̶／ +いたします |
| *o-yomi/m̶a̶s̶u̶/ itashimasu* | お読み／ま̶す̶／いたします |

In the humble polite form, the honorific prefix *o-* お- is added before the */-masu/* stem, which is then followed by the verb *suru* する (formal: *shimasu* します). For even greater humility, *suru* する can be replaced by its humble version *itasu* いたす (formal: *itashimasu* いたします).

### ■Examples

In the following example, the student uses a humble form when talking to the teacher. The humble form—not the honorific—is appropriate here because the verb refers to the student's own action.

学生：私がお手伝いします。 [手伝う *tetsudau*]
教師：それはありがたいな。

*Gakusei: Watashi ga o-tetsudai shimasu.*
*Kyōshi: Sore wa arigatai na.*
Student: I'll help you.
Teacher: I'm grateful for that.

Yamamoto uses the humble form to his boss:

山本：そのコンピュータでしたら、私が使い方をお教え
　　　いたします。 [教える *oshieru*]
課長：僕にもできるかな。

*Yamamoto: Sono kompyūta deshitara, watashi ga tsukai-kata o o-oshie itashimasu.*

*Kachō: Boku ni mo dekiru ka na.*

Yamamoto: If you need to use that computer, I can teach you how to operate it.

Section chief: I wonder if I can do it.

In the next two examples, service workers use the humble form when speaking to their customers.

旅行の添乗員：皆様のお写真をおとりしましょうか。[とる *toru*]

旅行者：お願いします。[願う *negau*]

*Ryokō no tenjō-in: Mina-sama no o-shashin o o-tori shi-mashō ka?*

*Ryokōsha: Onegai shimasu.*

Tour conductor: Shall I take a picture of you all?

Tourists: Please do.

花屋：明日の昼ごろ、ご自宅の方にお花をお届けいたします。[届ける *todokeru*]

お客：留守になるから、夕方お願いしたいんだけど。

*Hanaya: Myōnichi no hiru goro, go-jitaku no hō ni o-hana o o-todoke itashimasu.*

*O-kyaku: Rusu ni naru kara, yūgata onegai shitai n' da kedo.*

Florist: We'll deliver the flowers to your home around noon tomorrow.

Customer: I'll be out, so please deliver them in the early evening instead.

Note that the tourists and the customer at the florist's use *onegai suru* お願いする. Although in derivation this phrase is the humble form of the verb *negau* 願う, it has become a set expression for making polite requests. While these people would not use other humble forms when speaking to service workers, *onegai suru* お願いする and its variants *onegai shitai* お願いしたい and *onegai shimasu* お願いします are used in nearly all situations to mean "please do this for me."

## Irregular Honorific and Humble Forms 尊敬語と 謙譲語の特別形

The following table shows the verbs that have irregular honorific or humble forms. The honorific and humble forms are given in both the plain form and the /-masu/ form.

| Plain | Honorific | Humble |
|---|---|---|
| **to go** | | |
| *iku* 行く | *irassharu, irasshaimasu* いらっしゃる, いらっしゃいます *oide ni naru, oide ni narimasu* おいでになる, おいでになります | *mairu, mairimasu* まいる, まいります |
| **to come** | | |
| *kuru* 来る | *irassharu, irasshaimasu* いらっしゃる, いらっしゃいます *oide ni naru, oide ni narimasu* おいでになる, おいでになります | *mairu, mairimasu* まいる, まいります |
| **to be** | | |
| *iru* いる | *irassharu, irasshaimasu* いらっしゃる, いらっしゃいます *oide ni naru, oide ni narimasu* おいでになる, おいでになります | *oru, orimasu* おる, おります |
| **to eat** | | |
| *taberu* 食べる | *meshiagaru, meshiagarimasu* 召し上がる, 召し上がります | *itadaku, itadakimasu* いただく, いただきます |

Note: The previously nonstandard *otabe ni naru* お食べになる has now become frequently used.

| Plain | Honorific | Humble |
|---|---|---|
| to drink | | |
| *nomu*<br>飲む | *meshiagaru,*<br>    *meshiagarimasu*<br>召し上がる,<br>    召し上がります | *itadaku, itadaki-*<br>*masu*<br>いただく,<br>    いただきます |

Note: The previously nonstandard *onomi ni naru* お飲みになる has now become frequently used.

| Plain | Honorific | Humble |
|---|---|---|
| to say | | |
| *iu*<br>言う | *ossharu, osshaimasu*<br>おっしゃる,<br>    おっしゃいます | *mōsu, mōshimasu*<br>申す, 申します |
| to see | | |
| *miru*<br>見る | *goran ni naru,*<br>    *goran ni narimasu*<br>ご覧になる,<br>    ご覧になります | *haiken suru, haiken*<br>    *shimasu*<br>拝見する,<br>    拝見します |
| to know | | |
| *shitte iru*<br>知っている | *gozonji da,*<br>    *gozonji desu*<br>ご存じだ, ご存じです | *zonjite oru, zonjite*<br>    *orimasu*<br>存じておる,<br>    存じております |
| to do | | |
| *suru*<br>する | *nasaru, nasaimasu*<br>なさる, なさいます<br>*sareru, saremasu*<br>される, されます | *itasu, itashimasu*<br>いたす, いたします |
| to put on | | |
| *kiru*<br>着る | *o-meshi ni naru,*<br>    *o-meshi ni narimasu*<br>おめしになる,<br>    おめしになります | *kiru, kimasu*<br>着る, 着ます |
| to meet | | |
| *au*<br>会う | *o-ai ni naru,*<br>    *o-ai ni narimasu*<br>お会いになる,<br>    お会になります | *o-me ni kakaru, o-me*<br>    *ni kakarimasu*<br>お目にかかる,<br>    お目にかかります |
| to hear or ask | | |
| *kiku*<br>聞く | *o-kiki ni naru,*<br>    *o-kiki ni narimasu* | *ukagau,*<br>    *ukagaimasu* |

| Plain | Honorific | Humble |
|-------|-----------|--------|
| | お聞きになる,<br>　お聞きになります | 伺う, 伺います |

**to visit**

| Plain | Honorific | Humble |
|-------|-----------|--------|
| *tazuneru*<br>訪ねる | *o-tazune ni naru,*<br>　*o-tazune ni narimasu*<br>お訪ねになる,<br>　お訪ねになります | *ukagau,*<br>　*ukagaimasu*<br>伺う, 伺います |

**to die**

| Plain | Honorific | Humble |
|-------|-----------|--------|
| *shinu*<br>死ぬ | *o-nakunari ni naru,*<br>　*o-nakunari ni narimasu*<br>お亡くなりになる,<br>　お亡くなりになります | *shinu, shinimasu*<br><br>死ぬ, 死にます<br><br>*nakunaru,*<br>　*nakunarimasu*<br>亡くなる,<br>　亡くなります |

**to sleep**

| Plain | Honorific | Humble |
|-------|-----------|--------|
| *neru*<br>寝る | *o-yasumi ni naru,*<br>　*o-yasumi ni narimasu*<br>お休みになる,<br>　お休みになります | *yasumu,*<br>　*yasumimasu*<br>休む, 休みます |

**to give**

| Plain | Honorific | Humble |
|-------|-----------|--------|
| *ageru*<br>上げる | *o-age ni naru,*<br>　*o-age ni narimasu*<br>お上げになる,<br>　お上げになります | *sashiageru,*<br>　*sashiagemasu*<br>差し上げる,<br>　差し上げます |

**to receive**

| Plain | Honorific | Humble |
|-------|-----------|--------|
| *morau*<br>もらう | *o-morai ni naru,*<br>　*o-morai ni narimasu*<br><br>おもらいになる,<br>　おもらいになります | *itadaku, itadakimasu*<br>(giver not in<br>speaker's group)<br>いただく,<br>　いただきます |

**to give**

| Plain | Honorific | Humble |
|-------|-----------|--------|
| *kureru*<br>くれる | *kudasaru, kudasaimasu*<br>くださる, くださいます<br>(recipient in speaker's<br>group) | |

■ **Examples**

In the next two examples, Yamamoto uses the honorific form when talking to his superiors.

山本：今日は何時まで会社にいらっしゃいますか。[いる *iru*]

課長：夕方会議があるから、夜遅くまでいるよ。

*Yamamoto: Kyō wa nanji made kaisha ni irasshaimasu ka?*

*Kachō: Yūgata kaigi ga aru kara, yoru osoku made iru yo.*

Yamamoto: Until what time will you be at the company today?

Section chief: I have a meeting beginning in the early evening, so I'll be here until late.

山本：部長、今日は何を召し上がりますか。[食べる *taberu*]

部長：そうだね、久しぶりに寿司でも食べようか。

*Yamamoto: Buchō, kyō wa nani o meshiagarimasu ka?*

*Buchō: Sō da ne, hisashiburi ni sushi de mo tabeyō ka.*

Yamamoto: What would you like to eat today?

Division chief: Let me see. Maybe I'll have sushi. I haven't had that for a while.

In the next example, Yamamoto and the division chief use the humble *o-me ni kakaru* お目にかかる when speaking in reference to themselves and their meeting the company's vice-president, who is ranked above them both. When in reference to the vice-president and his actions, they use honorific forms (*ogenki* お元気, *ikareru* 行かれる, *go-shisatsu* 御視察, *ossharu* おっしゃる). Yamamoto also uses the honorific *nasaru* なさる when talking about the action of the division chief, who is his superior.

山本：きのうは本社で、佐藤副社長にお目にかかりました。[会う *au*]

部長：そう、それでお元気だった？

山本：ええ、なんでも月末にはヨーロッパへご視察に行かれるとか、おっしゃってましたよ。[行く *iku*, 言う *iu*]

部長：それじゃその前に、ちょっとお目にかかっておいた方がいいかな。

山本：そうなさった方がいいかも知れませんね。[する *suru*]

*Yamamoto: Kinō wa honsha de, Satō-fukushachō ni o-me
ni kakarimashita.*

*Buchō: Sō, sore de o-genki datta?*

*Yamamoto: Ē, nandemo getsumatsu ni wa Yōroppa e go-
shisatsu ni ikareru to ka, osshatte 'mashita yo.*

*Buchō: Sore ja sono mae ni, chotto o-me ni kakatte oita
hō ga ii ka na.*

*Yamamoto: Sō nasatta hō ga ii ka mo shiremasen ne.*

Yamamoto: Yesterday I met Vice-President Satō at company headquarters.

Division chief: Is that so? How was he?

Yamamoto: Fine. I understand that he's going to Europe
on an inspection trip at the end of this month.

Division chief: Then maybe I should drop in on him beforehand.

Yamamoto: That might be best.

## Giving and Receiving 授受の言い方

The forms for giving and receiving depend on the direction
of the action and the relations of group membership, respect,
and humility among the giver, receiver, and speaker.

### Formal Forms

| |
|---|
| A → B  A gives N to B. |
| *A wa B ni N o agemasu.*     A は B に N をあげます。 |
| B ← A  B receives N from A. |
| *B wa A ni N o moraimasu.*   B は A に N をもらいます。 |
| A → B  A gives N to B. |
| *A wa B ni N o kuremasu.*    A は B に N をくれます。 |

When the respect relation between the parties is not important, the verbs *ageru* あげる, *morau* もらう, and *kureru*
くれる are used to describe giving and receiving. The choice
of verb depends on whether or not the giver or recipient is in

the speaker's group (which, of course, includes the speaker).

If the recipient B is not in the speaker's group, then the following is possible. (The formal patterns appear on the left, the informal on the right.)

| | |
|---|---|
| *A wa B ni N o agemasu.* | *A wa B ni N o ageru* |
| A は B に N をあげます。 | A は B に N をあげる。 |
| A gives N to B. | A gives N to B. |

If A, the giver, is not in the speaker's group, then you can say:

| | |
|---|---|
| *B wa A ni N o moraimasu.* | *B wa A ni N o morau.* |
| B は A に N をもらいます。 | B は A に N をもらう。 |
| B receives N from A. | B receives N from A. |

In the following pattern, the recipient B must be in the speaker's group:

| | |
|---|---|
| *A wa B ni N o kuremasu.* | *A wa B ni N o kureru.* |
| A は B に N をくれます。 | A は B に N をくれる。 |
| A gives N to B. | A gives N to B. |

Another word meaning "give" is *yaru* やる. This somewhat brusque verb is used only when the recipient is much lower in status than the giver—typically, younger brothers or sisters, plants, and animals.

■ **Formal examples**

弟は田山さんに切手をあげました。
*Otōto wa Tayama-san ni kitte o agemashita.*
My younger brother gave some stamps to Ms. Tayama.

田山さんは弟に切手をもらいました。
*Tayama-san wa otōto ni kitte o moraimashita.*
Ms. Tayama received some stamps from my younger brother.

母は私に洋服をくれました。
*Haha wa watashi ni yōfuku o kuremashita.*
My mother gave me some clothes.

■ **Informal examples**

花に水をやった。

*Hana ni mizu o yatta.*
I gave some water to the flowers.

友達から結婚祝いにテレビをもらった。
*Tomodachi kara kekkon-iwai ni terebi o moratta.*
We received a television from our friends as a wedding present.

谷さんは私にケーキと花をくれた。
*Tani-san wa watashi ni kēki to hana o kureta.*
Tani gave me a cake and some flowers.

## The *-Te* Form

A → B   A does N for B.

*A wa B ni N o verb-te agemasu.*    A は B に N を <u>ーて</u> あげます。

B ← A   B receives (the favor) N from A.

*B wa A ni N o verb-te moraimasu*    B は A に N を <u>ーて</u> もらいます。

A → B   A does N for B.

*A wa B ni N o verb-te kuremasu.*    A は B に N を <u>ーて</u> くれます。

There are parallel patterns using the *-te* form to express the idea of one party doing a favor for another.

Here is "A does N for B" when B is not in the speaker's group:

*A wa B ni N o <u>verb-te</u> agemasu.*    A は B に N を <u>ーて</u> あげます。

Next, "B receives (the favor) N from A" when B and the speaker are in the same group and in a different group from A:

*B wa A ni N o <u>verb-te</u> moraimasu.*    B は A に N を <u>ーて</u> もらいます。

The third pattern is "A does N for B" when B and the speaker are in the same group:

*A wa B ni N o <u>verb-te</u> kuremasu.*　　A は B に N を <u>ーて</u>
　　　　　　　　　　　　　　　　　　くれます。

■ **Formal examples**

青木さんは友達にお金を貸してあげました。
*Aoki-san wa tomodachi ni o-kane o kashite agemashita.*
Ms. Aoki lent some money to a friend.

エリックさんは田村さんに京都を案内してもらいました。
*Erikku-san wa Tamura-san ni Kyōto o annai shite moraimashita.*
Eric was shown around Kyoto by Mr. Tamura.

母は私にセーターを編んでくれました。
*Haha wa watashi ni sētā o ande kuremashita.*
My mother knit a sweater for me.

■ **Informal examples**

きのう私は妹に料理を作ってあげた。
*Kinō watashi wa imōto ni ryōri o tsukutte ageta.*
Yesterday I cooked a meal for my little sister.

西さんはお父さんに新しい車を買ってもらった。
*Nishi-san wa otōsan ni atarashii kuruma o katte moratta.*
Mr. Nishi had a new car bought for him by his father.
　　(I.e., Nishi's father bought him a new car.)

友達は私に旅行の写真を見せてくれた。
*Tomodachi wa watashi ni ryokō no shashin o misete kureta.*
My friend showed me her travel photos.

## Polite and Humble Forms 敬語の文 ━━━━━

---

A → B　　A gives N to B.

　*A wa B ni N o sashiagemasu.*　A は B に N をさしあ
　　　　　　　　　　　　　　　　　げます。

B ← A　　B receives N from A.

　*B wa A ni N o itadakimasu.*　　B は A に N をいただ
　　　　　　　　　　　　　　　　　きます。

---

A → B    A gives N to B.

*A wa B ni N o kudasaimasu.*    A は B に N をくださ
います。

When the relative social positions of the parties come into
play, special respectful and humble forms are used. To say
"A gives N to B" when B is in a higher social position relative to A and the speaker, use the humble verb *sashiageru* さ
しあげる:

*A wa B ni N o sashiagemasu.*
A は B に N をさしあげます。
A gives N to B.

To say "B receives N from A" when B and the speaker
are in the same group and are in a lower social position than
A, use the humble verb *itadaku*  いただく:

*B wa A ni N o itadakimasu.*
B は A に N をいただきます。
B receives N from A.

To say "A gives N to B" when B and the speaker are in
the same group and are in a lower social position than A, use
the honorific verb *kudasaru* くださる:

*A wa B ni N o kudasaimasu.*
A は B に N をくださいます。
A gives N to B.

● Examples

村山さんは先生に、写真をさしあげました。
*Murayama-san wa sensei ni, shashin o sashiagemashita.*
Mr. Murayama gave a photograph to the teacher.

私は林教授に、本をいただきました。
*Watashi wa Hayashi-kyōju ni, hon o itadakimashita.*
I received a book from Professor Hayashi.

林教授は、私に本をくださいました。
*Hayashi-kyōju wa, watashi ni hon o kudasaimashita.*

Professor Hayashi gave me a book.

## ■ The *-Te* Form

> A → B    A does N for B.
>
> *A wa B ni N o <u>verb-te</u>*    A は B に N を <u>ーて</u>
> *sashiagemasu.*                   さしあげます。
>
> B ← A    B receives (the favor) N from A.
>
> *B wa A ni N o <u>verb-te</u>*    B は A に N を <u>ーて</u>
> *itadakimasu.*                    いただきます。
>
> A → B    A does N for B.
>
> *A wa B ni N o <u>verb-te</u>*    A は B に N を <u>ーて</u>
> *kudasaimasu.*                    くださいます。

The above polite patterns use the *-te* form to show that one party has done a favor for another. The first pattern means "A does N for B," when B is in a higher social position than both A and the speaker:

*A wa B ni N o <u>verb-te</u>*    A は B に N を <u>ーて</u>
*sashiagemasu.*                   さしあげます。

Next, "B receives (the favor) N from A." Here, B and the speaker are in the same group and are in a lower social position than A:

*B wa A ni N o <u>verb-te</u>*    B は A に N を <u>ーて</u>
*itadakimasu.*                    いただきます。

The third pattern is "A does N for B," with B and the speaker in the same group and in a lower social position than A.

*A wa B ni N o <u>verb-te</u>*    A は B に N を <u>ーて</u>
*kudasaimasu.*                    くださいます。

● Examples

私は社長に手紙を訳してさしあげました。
*Watashi wa shachō ni tegami o yakushite sashiagema-shita.*

I translated the letter for the president.

妹はジョンソン先生に、ピアノを教えていただきました。

*Imōto wa Jonson-sensei ni, piano o oshiete itadaki-mashita.*

My younger sister was taught piano by Ms. Johnson.

ジョンソン先生は、妹にピアノを教えてくださいました。

*Jonson-sensei wa, imōto ni piano o oshiete kudasai-mashita.*

Ms. Johnson taught piano to my younger sister.

## Asking for Permission 許可を求める言い方

Polite

> ... *sasete itadaite mo yoroshii deshō ka?*
>
> 〜させていただいてもよろしいでしょうか
>
> ... *sasete itadaite mo sashitsukae nai deshō ka?*
>
> 〜させていただいてもさしつかえないでしょうか

Formal

> ... *shite mo kamaimasen ka?*
>
> 〜してもかまいませんか
>
> ... *shite mo ii desu ka?*
>
> 〜してもいいですか
>
> ... *shite wa ikemasen ka?*
>
> 〜してはいけませんか

Informal

> ... *shite mo ii?*
>
> 〜してもいい？
>
> ... *shite wa dame?*
>
> 〜してはだめ？

## Polite

There are two patterns that can be used to ask for permission very politely. Both patterns employ the *-te* form of the causative verb (see page 83). The example structures use *sasete* させて, the *-te* form of *saseru* させる, which itself is the causative form of *suru* する. The first pattern literally means "Would it be acceptable for you to allow me to do ...?":

*... sasete itadaite mo yoroshii deshō ka?*
〜させていただいてもよろしいでしょうか

The second pattern literally means "Would it be no hindrance for you to allow me to do ...?"

*... sasete itadaite mo sashitsukae nai deshō ka?*
〜させていただいてもさしつかえないでしょうか

### ■ Examples

堀：この電話を使わせていただいてもよろしいでしょうか。 [使う *tsukau*]
山口：どうぞ、お使いください。

*Hori: Kono denwa o tsukawasete itadaite mo yoroshii deshō ka.*
*Yamaguchi: Dōzo, o-tsukai kudasai.*

Hori: May I have your permission to use this telephone?
Yamaguchi: Please go ahead and use it.

かぜを引いたので、明日の会に欠席させていただいてもさしつかえないでしょうか。 [する *suru*]

*Kaze o hiita no de, myōnichi no kai ni kesseki sasete itadaite mo sashitsukae nai deshō ka.*

I've caught a cold, so I wonder if it would not be a bother if you were to allow me to be absent from tomorrow's meeting.

## Formal

The next three patterns for asking permission are slightly less polite than those given above, though they are still suitable for most formal situations. They all use the *-te* form of the verb (in these examples it is して *shite*, the *-te* form of す

る *suru*). The first pattern could be translated literally as "Would you mind if I ...?":

> ... *shite mo kamaimasen ka?*　　〜してもかまいませんか。

The next pattern literally means "Would it be all right if I ...?":

> ... *shite mo ii desu ka?*　　　〜してもいいですか。

The direct meaning of the third pattern is "Would it be wrong to ~?":

> ... *shite wa ikemasen ka?*　　　〜してはいけませんか。

## ■ Examples

山田：ここに車を止めてもかまいませんか。 [止める
　　 *tomeru*]
店員：いいえ、あそこなら大丈夫ですよ。
*Yamada: Koko ni kuruma o tomete mo kamaimasen ka?*
*Ten'in: Īe, asoko nara daijōbu desu yo.*
Yamada: Would you mind if I parked my car here?
Shop employee: No, right there is fine.

Yamada could also have used the second or third patterns:

ここに車を止めてもいいですか。
*Koko ni kuruma o tomete mo ii desu ka?*
ここに車を止めてはいけませんか。
*Koko ni kuruma o tomete wa ikemasen ka?*

## Informal

The next two patterns are used between close acquaintances in informal situations. The first is the same as the second formal pattern above without the formal *desu ka* ですか. To mark it as a question, the phrase is pronounced with a rising intonation.

> ... *shite mo ii?*　　　　　〜してもいい？

The second pattern is also pronounced with a rising intonation. The literal meaning is "Is it wrong if I ...?"

> ...*shite wa dame?*　　　〜してはだめ？

■ **Example**

太郎：明日行ってもいい？ [行く *iku*]
花子：明日はだめ。
*Tarō: Ashita itte mo ii?*
*Hanako: Ashita wa dame.*
Taro: Okay if I come over tomorrow?
Hanako: Tomorrow's no good.

## Making an Invitation 相手を誘う言い方

Polite

  *o + /-masu/ + ni*
  *narimasen ka*

お／ま す／＋になりませんか

    *oyomi ni nari-*
    *masen ka*

お読みになりませんか
[読む *yomu*]

Formal

  */-masu/ + mashō*

／ー ま す／＋ましょう

    *iki/masu/mashō*

行き／ま す／ましょう
[行く *iku*]

  */-masu/ + mashō ka*

／ー ま す／＋ましょうか

    *iki/masu/mashō ka*

行き／ま す／ましょうか

  */-masu/ + masen ka*

／ー ま す／＋ませんか

    *iki/masu/masen ka*

行き／ま す／ませんか

Informal

  ① */-u/ + ō*

    *ik/u/ō*

行こう [行く *iku*]

  ② */-ru/ + yō*

／ー る／＋よう

    *mi/ru/yō*

見／る／よう [見る *miru*]

  ③ *kuru → koyō*

来る → 来よう

    *suru → shiyō*

する → しよう

## Polite

To make a polite invitation, use the honorific polite form *o* + /-~~masu~~/ + *ni naru*, changing the final *naru* なる to the formal negative question *narimasen ka* なりませんか.

> *O-yomi ni narimasen ka.*　　　お読みになりませんか。
> 　　　　　　　　　　　　　　　[読む *yomu*]
>
> Would you like to read (this)?

### ■ Example

小川：いっしょにビールをお飲みになりませんか。[飲む *nomu*]
教師：いいですね。飲みましょう。

*Ogawa: Issho ni bīru o o-nomi ni narimasen ka.*
*Kyōshi: Ii desu ne. Nomimashō.*

Ogawa: Would you like to go and have a beer together?
Teacher: That'd be nice. Let's do that.

## Formal

One way to make an invitation in a formal conversation is change the *-masu* ーます suffix to *-mashō* ーましょう. This is called the formal volitional form of the verb. Thus 行きます becomes:

> *Ikimashō.*　　　　　　　行きましょう。[行く *iku*]
> Let's go.

The question marker *ka* か can be added to make the invitation a bit less direct.

> *Ikimashō ka.*　　　　　　行きましょうか。
> Shall we go?

You can also use the formal negative (*-masen*) followed by *ka*.

> *Ikimasen ka.*　　　　　　行きませんか。
> Wouldn't you like to go?

### ■ Examples

いっしょに映画を見ましょう。
*Issho ni eiga o mimashō.*

Let's see a movie together.

いっしょに映画を見ましょうか。
*Issho ni eiga o mimashō ka.*
Shall we see a movie together?

いっしょに映画を見ませんか。
*Issho ni eiga o mimasen ka?*
Wouldn't you like to see a movie together?

## Informal

Between friends, the informal volitional form can be used. This is formed as follows:

① Change the final -*u* of the plain form to *ō*:

*iku* → *ikō*　　　　行く → 行こう
*tatsu* → *tatō*　　　立つ → 立とう

　　Note: Final *tsu* changes to *tō*.

② Change the final -*ru* of the plain form to *yō*:

*miru* → *miyō*　　　見る → 見よう

③ *kuru* → *koyō*　　来る → 来よう
*suru* → *shiyō*　　　する → しよう

### ■ Examples

いっしょに映画を見よう。
*Issho ni eiga o miyō.*
Let's see a movie together.

It's also possible to use the plain negative (-*nai*) form with a rising tone, so you could also say:

いっしょに映画を見ない？
*Issho ni eiga o minai?*
Do you wanna see a movie?

## Expressing Intention　意志を表す言い方

The following describes two techniques for expressing one's intention to do something. The first uses the word *tsumori*

つもり, while the second uses the volitional form plus the verbs *omou* 思う or *kangaeru* 考える "to think."

## Tsumori つもり

---

> Formal
> > plain form + *tsumori desu*      原形 + つもりです
> > > *kiku tsumori desu*              聞くつもりです
>
> Informal
> > plain form + *tsumori*        原形 + つもり
> > > *yomu tsumori*                 読むつもり
> > plain form + *tsumori da*     原形 + つもりだ
> > > *kuru tsumori da*              来るつもりだ

In formal situations, use the plain form of the verb followed by *tsumori desu* つもりです:

> *Kiku tsumori desu.*      聞くつもりです。
> I intend to listen.

In informal situations, the copula *desu* です can be replaced by *da* だ or omitted entirely.

> *Kiku tsumori da.*       聞くつもりだ。
> I intend to listen.

### ■ Examples

山本：いつアメリカへ行きますか。
中田：来年行くつもりです。
*Yamamoto: Itsu Amerika e ikimasu ka.*
*Nakata: Rainen iku tsumori desu.*
Yamamoto: When are you going to America?
Nakata: I plan to go next year.

In the next example, Ms. Satō drops the copula altogether and employs a rising intonation for her question. Ms. Tanaka replies with the feminine explanatory ending *na no* なの.

佐藤：今晩、どんな料理作るつもり？
田中：今晩は外で食べるつもりなの。

*Satō: Komban, donna ryōri tsukuru tsumori?*
*Tanaka: Komban wa soto de taberu tsumori na no.*
Satō: What do you plan to cook this evening?
Tanaka: I plan to eat out tonight.

## With Volitional Verbs 推量形 ━━━━━━

Formal

① /ﾑ/ + ō to omoimasu, omotte imasu, kangaete imasu

    *nomō to omotte imasu*      飲もうと思ってい
                                  ます [飲む *nomu*]

② /ﾙ/ + yō to omoimasu, omotte imasu, kangaete imasu

    *dekakeyō to omotte imasu*    出かけようと思って
                                    います [出かける
                                    *dekakeru*]

③ *shiyō to omoimasu, shiyō*     しようと思います、し
    *to omotte imasu*            ようと思っています

    *koyō to omoimasu, koyō*    来ようと思います、来
    *to omotte imasu*            ようと思っています

Informal

    *-ō, -yō to omou, omotte*      ―おう、―ようと思う、思
    *iru, kangaete iru*          っている、考えている

    *ikō to omou*                行こうと思う

When the verbs *omou* 思う and *kangaeru* 考える are used to express intention, they follow the informal volitional form (see page 57) plus *to* と. These verbs make the speaker's intention seem less definite than with *tsumori* つもり. In this construction, *omou* 思う can be used either in the present tense (formal *omoimasu* 思います and informal *omou* 思う) or the present continuous (formal *omotte imasu* 思っています, informal *omotte iru* 思っている). However, *kangaeru* 考える is used only in the present continuous (formal *kangaete imasu* 考えています, informal *kangaete iru* 考えている). In these usages, the two words are basically interchangeable, although *omou* 思う in its various forms is more widely used.

Here are the formal versions with the verb *nomu* 飲む "to drink." Its informal volitional form is *nomō* 飲もう.

| | |
|---|---|
| *Nomō to omoimasu.*<br>飲もうと思います。<br>I think I'll drink. | *Nomō to omotte imasu.*<br>飲もうと思っています。<br>I'm thinking of drinking. |
| — | *Nomō to kangaete imasu.*<br>飲もうと考えています。<br>I'm thinking of drinking. |

Here are the informal versions:

| | |
|---|---|
| *Nomō to omou.*<br>飲もうと思う。<br>I think I'll drink. | *Nomō to omotte iru.*<br>飲もうと思っている。<br>I'm thinking of drinking. |
| — | *Nomō to kangaete iru.*<br>飲もうと考えている。<br>I'm thinking of drinking. |

## ■ Formal example

教師：大学を卒業したら、どうするんですか。
学生：卒業したら、大学院に行こうと考えています。[行く *iku*]
*Kyōshi: Daigaku o sotsugyō shitara, dō suru n' desu ka.*
*Gakusei: Sotsugyō shitara, daigakuin ni ikō to kangaete imasu.*
Teacher: What are you going to do after you graduate from college?
Student: After I graduate, I'm thinking of going to graduate school.

## ■ Informal example

花子：日曜日、何するつもり？
太郎：歌舞伎見ようと思ってる。[見る *miru*]
*Hanako: Nichiyōbi, nani suru tsumori?*
*Tarō: Kabuki miyō to omotte 'ru.*

Hanako: What do you plan to do on Sunday?
Tarō: I'm thinking of going to see Kabuki.

## Expressing Wishes 希望や願望を表す言い方

*-Tai* ーたい

Formal

| | |
|---|---|
| /-~~masu~~/ + *tai desu* | ／ー~~ます~~／＋たいです |
| *iki*/~~masu~~/*tai desu* | 行き／~~ます~~／たいです |
| /-~~masu~~/ + *tai to omoimasu* | ／ー~~ます~~／＋たいと思います |
| *iki*/~~masu~~/*tai to omoimasu* | 行き／~~ます~~／たいと思います |
| /-~~masu~~/ + *tai to omotte imasu* | ／ー~~ます~~／＋たいと思っています |
| *iki*/~~masu~~/*tai to omotte imasu* | 行き／~~ます~~／たいと思っています |
| *-te mitai desu* | ーて＋みたいです |
| *itte mitai desu* | 行ってみたいです |
| *-te mitai to omoimasu* | ーて＋みたいと思います |
| *itte mitai to omoimasu* | 行ってみたいと思います |

Informal

| | |
|---|---|
| /-~~masu~~/ + *tai* | ／ー~~ます~~／＋たい |
| *iki*/~~masu~~/*tai* | 行き／~~ます~~／たい |
| /-~~masu~~/ + *tai to omou* | ／ー~~ます~~／＋たいと思う |
| *iki*/~~masu~~/*tai to omou* | 行き／~~ます~~／たいと思う |
| /-~~masu~~/ + *tai to omotte iru* | ／ー~~ます~~／＋たいと思っている |
| *iki*/~~masu~~/*tai to omotte iru* | 行き／~~ます~~／たいと思っている |

Third Person

| *-tai → -tagaru* | ―たい → ―たがる |
| *tabetai → tabetagaru* | 食べたい → 食べたがる |

The *-tai* form is used to express wishes and desires in the first and second person. Add *-tai* ―たい to the *-masu* form:

*tabe/~~masu~~/tai*　食べ／~~ます~~／たい

In formal situations, the *-tai* form is followed by *desu* です, by *to omoimasu* と思います, or by *to omotte imasu* と思っています.

| *Tabetai desu.* | 食べたいです。 |
| I want to eat. | |
| *Tabetai to omoimasu.* | 食べたいと思います。 |
| I'd like to eat. | |
| *Tabetai to omotte imasu.* | 食べたいと思っています。 |
| I am thinking of eating (I hope to eat). | |

To say that you want to try something, use the *-te* form of the verb followed by *mitai* みたい. This pattern is often used when trying something for the first time.

| *Sore o tabete mitai desu.* | それを食べてみたいです。 |
| I'd like to try that. | |
| *Sore o tabete mitai to omoimasu.* | それを食べてみたいと思います。 |
| I think I'd like to try that. | |
| *Sore o tabete mitai to omotte imasu.* | それを食べてみたいと思っています。 |
| I am thinking of trying that. | |

In informal situations, the *-tai* form is followed by nothing, by *to omou* と思う, or by *to omotte iru* と思っている:

| *Tabetai.* | 食べたい。 |
| I want to eat. | |
| *Tabetai to omou.* | 食べたいと思う。 |
| I think I'd like to eat. | |
| *Tabetai to omotte iru.* | 食べたいと思っている。 |

I'm thinking of eating.

■ **Formal examples**

園田：夏休みに何をしますか。
佐瀬：シンガポールへ行ってみたいですね。

*Sonoda: Natsu yasumi ni nani o shimasu ka.*
*Sase: Shingapōru e itte mitai desu ne.*

Sonoda: What are you going to do during summer vacation?
Sase: I'd like to go to Singapore.

Ms. Sase could also say:

シンガポールへ行ってみたいと思っています。

*Shingapōru e itte mitai to omotte imasu.*
I'm thinking that I'd like to go and see Singapore.

■ **Informal examples**

園田：休みに何するの？
佐瀬：シンガポールへ行ってみたい。

*Sonoda: Yasumi ni nani suru no?*
*Sase: Shingapōru e itte mitai.*

Sonoda: What'll you be doing during the vacation?
Sase: I want to go to Singapore.

Or:

シンガポールへ行ってみたいと思ってる。

*Shingapōru e itte mitai to omotte 'ru.*
I'm thinking I'd like to go and see Singapore.

## *-Tagaru* ーたがる

The *-tai* form is used primarily when speaking in the first or second person. When talking about a third party's desires or wishes, replace *-tai* ーたい with *-tagaru* ーたがる.

*tabetai* → *tabetagaru*     食べたい → 食べたがる [食
                                         べる *taberu*]

The *-tagaru* form is a Group 1 verb, so the *-masu* form of *tabetagaru* 食べたがる is *tabetagarimasu* 食べたがります and the *-te* form is *tabetagatte* 食べたがって.

**■ Examples**

子供は甘いものを食べたがります。
*Kodomo wa amai mono o tabetagarimasu.*
Children are always wanting to eat sweet things.

弟は新しい車を買いたがっています。
*Otōto wa atarashii kuruma o kaitagatte imasu.*
My younger brother wants to buy a new car.

### *To ii* といい

Formal

plain form + *to ii desu (ne)* 原形 + といいです (ね)
*hareru to ii desu ne* 晴れるといいですね

Informal

plain form + *to ii (ne, nā)* 原形 + といい (ね, なあ)
*hareru to ii ne* 晴れるといいね

To express a general wish or desire, use the plain form followed by *to ii desu (ne)* といいです(ね) in formal situations or *to ii (ne, nā)* といい(ね, なあ) in informal situations:

*Ame ga hareru to ii desu ne.* 雨が晴れるといいですね。
*Ame ga hareru to ii ne.* 雨が晴れるといいね。
It'd be nice if it stopped raining.

## Conditionals 仮定を表す言い方

There are two main strategies for expressing the idea of "if" in Japanese: the *-ba* form and the *-tara* form.

### *-Ba* ばの形

① */-~~u~~/ + eba*
*nom/-~~u~~/ + eba → nomeba* 飲む → 飲めば

Note: *tatsu* → *tateba*　　立つ → 立てば

② /-ʉ/ + *eba*

　　*taber/-ʉ/ + eba* → *tabereba*　食べる → 食べれば

③ *kuru* →*kureba*　　来る → 来れば

　　*suru* →*sureba*　　する → すれば

To make the *-ba* conditional form, drop the final *-u* of the plain form and add *-eba*.

■ **Examples**

雨が降れば涼しくなりますよ。
*Ame ga fureba suzushiku narimasu yo.*
If it rains, it'll become cooler.

酒を飲めば運転できない。
*Sake o nomeba unten dekinai.*
If I drink, I can't drive.

## *-Tara* 一たら

①, ② *-ta + ra*　　／一た／ + ら

　　*nonda* → *nondara*　飲んだ → 飲んだら [飲む *nomu*]

　　*tabeta* → *tabetara*　食べた → 食べたら [食べる *taberu*]

③ *kita* → *kitara*　　来た → 来たら [来る *kuru*]

　　*shita* → *shitara*　　した → したら [する *suru*]

The *-tara* form is derived by adding *-ra* 一ら to the informal past tense (*-ta*) form.

■ **Formal examples**

田中：練習したら上手になりますか。
佐藤：もちろん、上手になりますよ。
*Tanaka: Renshū shitara jōzu ni narimasu ka.*

*Satō: Mochiron, jōzu ni narimasu yo.*
Tanaka: If I practice, will I get better?
Satō: Of course you will.

■ **Informal examples**

練習したらうまくなるよ。
*Renshū shitara umaku naru yo.*
If you practice, you'll get better.

## Restrictions on *-ba*

Note that the *-ba* form cannot be followed by commands, requests, or suggestions. In those cases, use *-tara* instead.

■ **Incorrect**

京都に行けばおみやげを買って来て下さい。
*Kyōto ni ikeba omiyage o katte kite kudasai.*

明日雨が降れば、ゴルフはやめた方がいいでしょう。
*Ashita ame ga fureba, gorufu wa yameta hō ga ii deshō.*

■ **Correct**

京都に行ったらおみやげを買って来て下さい。
*Kyōto ni ittara omiyage o katte kite kudasai.*
If you go to Kyōto, buy a souvenir for me.

明日雨が降ったら、ゴルフはやめた方がいいでしょう。
*Ashita ame ga futtara, gorufu wa yameta hō ga ii deshō.*
If it rains tomorrow, you should cancel the golf.

# Expressing Requirements and Obligations
## 義務を表す言い方

| Formal | |
|---|---|
| /-~~nai~~/ + *nakereba narimasen* | /-~~ない~~/ + なければ なりません |

| | |
|---|---|
| *ika/~~nai~~/nakereba narimasen* | 行か/~~ない~~/なけれ<br>ばなりません |
| */-~~nai~~/ + nakereba ikemasen* | /―~~ない~~/ + なければ<br>いけません |
| *ika/~~nai~~/nakeraba ikemasen* | 行か/~~ない~~/→行な<br>ければいけません |

Informal

| | |
|---|---|
| */-~~nai~~/ + nakereba naranai* | /―~~ない~~/ + なければ<br>ならない |
| *ika/~~nai~~/nakereba naranai* | 行か/~~ない~~/なけれ<br>ばならない |
| */-~~nai~~/ + nakereba ikenai* | /―~~ない~~/ + なければ<br>いけない |
| *ika/~~nai~~/nakereba ikenai* | 行か/~~ない~~/なけれ<br>ばいけない |

Colloquial Speech

| | |
|---|---|
| */-~~nai~~/ + nakucha* | /―~~ない~~/ + なくちゃ |
| *ika/~~nai~~/nakucha* | 行か/~~ない~~/なくちゃ |
| */-~~nai~~/ + nakerya* | /―~~ない~~/ + なけりゃ |
| *ika/~~nai~~/nakerya* | 行か/~~ない~~/なけりゃ |

To express "have to," "must," or "should," use the */-nai/*
stem followed by *nakereba naranai* なければならない (formal: *nakereba narimasen* なければなりません) or *nakereba
ikenai* なければいけない (formal: *nakereba ikemasen* なけれ
ばいけません). Here are the forms for *suru* する:

| | |
|---|---|
| *shinai → shinakereba naranai* | しない → しなければ<br>ならない |
| → *shinakereba narimasen* | → しなければなりません |
| → *shinakereba ikenai* | → しなければいけない |
| → *shinakereba ikemasen* | → しなければいけません |

It's also possible to replace *-nakereba* with *-nakute wa*:

*shinakute wa naranai* しなくてはならない

In colloquial speech, the ending may become *nakucha* な
くちゃ or *nakerya* なけりゃ.

## Examples

石田：明日は８時の新幹線に乗らなければなりません。
　　　[乗る *noru*]
渡部：じゃ今晩は早く寝た方がいいですね。
石田：ええ、でも今晩中に今日の会議の報告を書かなく
　　　てはならないんですよ。[書く *kaku*]
渡部：それは大変ですね。

*Ishida: Ashita wa hachiji no Shinkansen ni noranakereba*
　　　*narimasen.*
*Watanabe: Ja komban wa hayaku neta hō ga ii desu ne.*
*Ishida: Ē, demo komban-jū ni kyō no kaigi no hōkoku o*
　　　*kakanakute wa naranai n' desu yo.*
*Watanabe: Sore wa taihen desu ne.*

Ishida: I have to take the Shinkansen tomorrow at eight.
Watanabe: Then you should get to bed early tonight.
Ishida: I know, but sometime tonight I have to write up a
　　　report on today's meeting.
Watanabe: That's really tough.

もう九時だ。すぐ行かなくちゃ。[行く *iku*]
*Mō kuji da. Sugu ikanakucha.*
It's already nine. We have to get going.

---

## Describing a Past Experience 経験を表す言い方

| | |
|---|---|
| *-ta + koto ga aru* | ―た＋ことがある |
| *atta koto ga aru* | 会ったことがある |

To say that one has done something in the past, use the
informal past tense (*-ta*) form followed by *koto ga aru* こと
がある (formal: *koto ga arimasu* ことがあります).

## Examples

広瀬：タイへ行ったことがありますか。 [行く *iku*]
久保：まだ行ったことがないんですよ。一度行って見た
　　　いんですけどね。

*Hirose: Tai e itta koto ga arimasu ka.*
*Kubo: Mada itta koto ga nai n' desu yo. Ichido itte mitai*
*n' desu kedo ne.*

Hirose: Have you ever been to Thailand?
Kubo: Not yet, but I'd like to go sometime.

石井：インド料理を食べたことがありますか。[食べる
　　　*taberu*]
山崎：一度だけ食べました。辛かったですよ。

*Ishii: Indo ryōri o tabeta koto ga arimasu ka.*
*Yamazaki: Ichido dake tabemashita. Karakatta desu yo.*

Ishii: Have you ever eaten Indian food?
Yamazaki: Just once. It was really spicy.

# Describing a Habitual Action　習慣を表す言い方

| | |
|---|---|
| (1) plain form + *koto mo aru* | 原形 + こともある |
| 　　*miru koto mo aru* | 見ることもある |
| (2) plain form + *koto ni shite iru* | 原形 + ことにしている |
| 　　*yomu koto ni shite iru* | 読むことにしている |
| (3) ... *-tari* ... *-tari suru* | 〜ー たり〜ーたりする |
| 　　*tabetari nondari suru* | 食べたり飲んだりする |

Here are the three ways to describe a habitual or repeated
action.

## (1) *Koto mo aru*　こともある

To say that you do something occasionally, use the plain
form followed by *koto mo aru* こともある (formal: *koto mo
arimasu* こともあります).

### ■ Formal examples

時々朝ご飯を食べずに会社へ行くこともあります。

*Tokidoki asagohan o tabezu ni kaisha e iku koto mo arimasu.*

Sometimes I go to work without eating breakfast.

### ■ Informal examples

日曜日はテニスをすることもある。

*Nichiyōbi wa tenisu o suru koto mo aru.*

I occasionally play tennis on Sundays.

## (2) *Koto ni shite iru* ことにしている

To say that you consciously make a habit of doing something, use the plain form followed by *koto ni shite iru* ことにしている (formal: *koto ni shite imasu* ことにしています). This can often be translated as "make a point of doing":

*hashiru koto ni shite iru*
走ることにしている
to make a point of running

### ■ Formal example

毎朝駅まで歩いて行くことにしています。

*Mai-asa eki made aruite iku koto ni shite imasu.*

I make a point of walking to the station every morning.

### ■ Informal example

個人的な手紙は、タイプではなく手で書くことにしている。

*Kojin-teki na tegami wa, taipu de wa naku te de kaku koto ni shite iru.*

I make a point of writing personal letters by hand, not typing them.

## (3) ... -*Tari* ... -*tari suru* 〜ーたり〜ーたりする

To say that there are several things you do habitually, add -*ri* ーり to the informal past tense (-*ta*) forms of the verbs, with the last verb followed by *suru* する (formal: *shimasu* します):

*tabeta, nonda*        食べた、飲んだ

*tabetari nondari suru*　　食べたり飲んだりする
to eat, drink, etc.

■ **Example**

山本：休みの日には、どんなことをなさっているんで
　　　すか。
課長：そうですね、テレビを見たり本を読んだりしてい
　　　ますね。

*Yamamoto: Yasumi no hi ni wa, donna koto o nasatte iru n'*
*desu ka.*
*Kachō: Sō desu ne, terebi o mitari hon o yondari shite*
*imasu ne.*

Yamamoto: What sorts of things do you do on your days
off?
Section chief: Well, I watch TV, read books—things like
that.

## Expressing Ability　可能な表現

There are two main strategies for saying that one is able to
do something, the pattern *koto ga dekiru* ことができる and
the potential form.

### *Koto ga dekiru*　ことができる

| | |
|---|---|
| plain form + *koto ga dekiru* | 原形 + ことができる |
| *iku koto ga dekiru* | 行くことができる |
| to be able to go | |

The plain form of the verb is followed by *koto ga dekiru*
ことができる (formal: *koto ga dekimasu* ことができます):

■ **Formal example**

電話で予約することができますか。
*Denwa de yoyaku suru koto ga dekimasu ka.*
Can you make reservations by telephone?

## ■ Informal example

電話で予約することができる。
*Denwa de yoyaku suru koto ga dekiru.*
You can make reservations by telephone.

Note that in reference to sports and language the form
<u>noun</u> *ga dekiru* is often used. For example,

英語ができますか。
*Eigo ga dekimasu ka.*
Can you (do you) speak English?

## Potential Form

---

① /-ʉ/ + *eru*

    ik/ʉ/ + *eru* → *ikeru*      行く→行ける

② /-ɾʉ/ + *rareru*      /ー呑/ + られる

    tabe/ɾʉ/*rareru*      食べ/呑/られる

③    *kuru* → *korareru*      来る → 来られる

     *suru* → *dekiru*      する → できる

---

Another way to express ability is with the verb's potential
form, which is derived as follows:

① Drop the final *-u* of the plain form and add *-eru*:

    *iku* → *ikeru*      行く → 行ける

    *tatsu* → *tateru*      立つ → 立てる

        Note that final *-tsu* becomes *-te.*

② Drop the final *-ru* ーる of the plain form and add *-rareru*
ーられる:

    *taberu* → *taberareru*      食べる → 食べられる

③    *kuru* → *korareru*      来る → 来られる

     *suru* → *dekiru*      する → できる

## ■ Example

鈴木：明日は早く来られますか。[来る *kuru*]
部長：早く来られるけど、何かあるの？
*Suzuki: Ashita wa hayaku koraremasu ka.*

*Buchō: Hayaku korareru kedo, nani ka aru no?*
Suzuki: Can you come early tomorrow?
Division chief: Yes, I can. What's up?

## ■ Note 1: The Changing Potential Form

Recently many people omit the *ra* ら from the potential suffix for Group 1 verbs and the irregular verb *kuru* 来る, producing:

*tabereru* 食べれる (instead of *taberareru* 食べられる)
*koreru* 来れる (instead of *korareru* 来られる)

Although this shorter form is frowned upon by some grammarians, it has become common in speech, especially among young people, and is even seen in informal writing such as advertising copy. The following are some typical examples from casual conversations:

知子：この映画見たいんだけど、もう遅いわね。
次郎：大丈夫、今からでも見れるよ。 [見る *miru*]
*Tomoko: Kono eiga mitai n' da kedo, mō osoi wa ne.*
*Jirō: Daijōbu, ima kara de mo mireru yo.*
Tomoko: I want to see this movie, but it's already too late.
Jirō: It's okay. There is still time to see it.

松本：それ、生で食べれるの？ [食べる *taberu*]
越智：食べれるよ。
*Matsumoto: Sore, nama de tabereru no?*
*Ochi: Tabereru yo.*
Matsumoto: Can you eat that raw?
Ochi: Sure you can.

## ■ Note 2: The Praising Potential

In colloquial speech, some potential verbs such as *ikeru* いける and *hanaseru* 話せる may indicate that something is good or worthwhile.

この酒、なかなかいけるじゃない。 [いく *iku*]
*Kono sake, nakanaka ikeru ja nai.*
This saké is pretty good, huh?

今度の課長、話せるのよ。[話す *hanasu*]
*Kondo no kachō, hanaseru no yo.*

The new section chief is someone you can talk to.

田中という新人は使えそうだね。[使う *tsukau*]
*Tanaka to iu shinjin wa tsukaesō da ne.*
It looks like that new employee Tanaka will work out well.

そのボールペン、書けますか。[書く *kaku*]
*Sono bōrupen, kakemasu ka.*
Does that ballpoint pen write well?

---

# Transitive and Intransitive Verbs
## 他動詞と自動詞

---

Many Japanese verbs can be grouped into transitive/intransitive pairs. Most verbs ending in *-su* are transitive, but otherwise there are no hard-and-fast rules for forming transitive verbs from intransitive verbs or vice versa. The following table shows several common patterns.

| Pattern | Intransitive | Transitive |
|---|---|---|
| *-u* → *-eru* | *aku* 開く to open, to be opened | *akeru* 開ける to open |
| | *tsuku* つく to be stuck to | *tsukeru* つける to stick to |
| | *muku* 向く to turn toward | *mukeru* 向ける to turn toward |
| *-u* → *-asu* | *ugoku* 動く to move | *ugokasu* 動かす to move |
| | *tobu* 飛ぶ to fly | *tobasu* 飛ばす to set flying |
| | *naku* 泣く to cry | *nakasu* 泣かす to make (someone) cry |
| *-u* → *-wasu* | *au* 合う to match | *awasu* 合わす to match |
| | *mau* 舞う to dance | *mawasu* 舞わす to cause to dance |
| *-iru* → *-osu* | *okiru* 起きる to get up | *okosu* 起こす to rouse |
| | *ochiru* 落ちる to fall | *otosu* 落とす to drop |
| | *oriru* 降りる to get down | *orosu* 降ろす to lower |

| Pattern | Intransitive | Transitive |
|---|---|---|
| *-eru → -asu* | *akeru* 明ける to become light | *akasu* 明かす to reveal |
| | *nigeru* 逃げる to flee | *nigasu* 逃がす to let go |
| *-eru → -yasu* | *hieru* 冷える to become cool | *hiyasu* 冷やす to make cool |
| | *fueru* 増える to increase | *fuyasu* 増やす to increase |
| | *moeru* 燃える to burn | *moyasu* 燃やす to set fire to |
| *-reru → -rasu* | *areru* 荒れる to be devastated | *arasu* 荒らす to devastate |
| | *okureru* 遅れる to be late | *okurasu* 遅らす to delay |
| *-aru → -eru* | *agaru* 上がる to rise | *ageru* 上げる to raise |
| | *atsumaru* 集まる to collect | *atsumeru* 集める to collect |
| | *sagaru* 下がる to drop | *sageru* 下げる to lower |
| *-waru → -eru* | *kawaru* 変わる to change | *kaeru* 変える to change |
| | *suwaru* 据わる to be set down | *sueru* 据える to set down |
| | *tsutawaru* 伝わる to be conveyed | *tsutaeru* 伝える to convey |
| *-eru → -u* | *oreru* 折れる to be broken | *oru* 折る to break |
| | *ureru* 売れる to be sold | *uru* 売る to sell |
| | *nugeru* 脱げる to come off | *nugu* 脱ぐ to take off |

## Using Transitive and Intransitive Verbs in Sentences
### 他動詞と自動詞の用法

The basic structure of a sentence with an intransitive verb is:

> subject + *ga* + verb

Transitive verbs (with the subject often omitted) take direct objects. The basic sentence pattern is:

> (subject +) direct object + *o* + verb

The subjects of intransitive verbs are often inanimate objects, while the subjects of transitive verbs are almost always people, organizations, animals, or other animate objects.

These patterns are summarized in the following table:

|  | Intransitive | Transitive |
|---|---|---|
| Particle | *ga* が | *o* を |
| Direct object | No | Yes |
| Subject | Often things | Usually people or groups |
| Verb suffix |  | Almost all verbs ending in *-su* ーす are transitive. |
| Basic sentence pattern | Subject + *ga* + verb | Subject + direct object + *o* + verb |

In the following examples, the pronoun *watashi* 私 is assumed to be the subject of the sentence when no subject is stated in Japanese. In context, of course, the actual subject may be different.

**Intransitive**

*To ga aku.*
戸が開く。
The door opens.

*To ga shimaru.*
戸が閉まる。
The door closes.

*Kaze ga hairu.*
風が入る。
The wind gets in.

**Transitive**

*To o akeru.*
戸を開ける。
I open the door.

*To o shimeru.*
戸を閉める。
I shut the door.

*Kūki o ireru.*
空気を入れる。
I let the air in.

| **Intransitive** | **Transitive** |
|---|---|

*Mizu ga deru.*
水が出る。
Water comes out (of the faucet).

*Mizu o dasu.*
水を出す。
I let the water out (of the faucet).

*(Watashi ga) densha ni noru.*
（私が）電車に乗る。
I get on the train.

*Nimotsu o noseru.*
荷物をのせる。
I put luggage (onto the train).

*Ie ga tatsu.*
家が建つ。
The houses are built.

*Ie o tateru.*
家を建てる。
I build houses.

*Mizu ga nagareru.*
水が流れる。
The water flows.

*Mizu o nagasu.*
水を流す。
I drain the water.

*Mise ga narabu.*
店が並ぶ。
The stores are in a row.

*Sara o naraberu.*
皿を並べる。
I line up the plates.

*Denki ga tsuku.*
電気がつく。
The (electric) light turns on.

*Denki o tsukeru.*
電気をつける。
I turn on the (electric) light.

*Akari ga kieru.*
明りが消える。
The light goes out.

*Akari o kesu.*
明りを消す。
I put out the light.

*(Watashi ga) asa okiru.*
（私が）朝起きる。
I get up in the morning.

*Kodomo o okosu.*
子供を起こす。
I wake up the children.

*Gakkō ga hajimaru.*
学校が始まる。
School begins.

*Shigoto o hajimeru.*
仕事を始める。
I begin work.

*Eiga ga owaru.*
映画が終る。
The film ends.

*Shukudai o oeru.*
宿題を終える。
I finish the homework.

*Kuruma ga tomaru.*
車が止まる。
The car stops.

*Kuruma o tomeru.*
車を止める。
I stop the car.

| **Intransitive** | **Transitive** |
|---|---|

*Keshiki ga utsuru.*

景色が写る。

The scenery appears (in the photo).

*Ji o utsusu.*

字を写す。

I copy the characters.

*Hi ga moeru.*

火が燃える。

The fire burns.

*Kami o moyasu.*

紙を燃やす。

I burn the paper.

Some further examples with longer sentences.

*Kaze de to ga akimashita.*

風で戸が開きました。
[開く *aku*]

The door blew open because of the wind.

*Atsui kara to o akete kudasai.*

暑いから戸を開けて下さい。
[開ける *akeru*]

It's hot, so please open the door.

*Ano heya no denki ga tsukimashita.*

あの部屋の電気がつきました。

[つく *tsuku*]

The lights turned on in that room.

*Yamada-san ga kūrā o tsukemashita.*

山田さんがクーラーをつけました。
[つける *tsukeru*]

Mr. Yamada turned on the air conditioner.

*Ie no mae de kuruma ga tomatta.*

家の前で車が止まった。
[止まる *tomaru*]

A car stopped in front of the house.

*Sono kado de kuruma o tomete kudasai.*

その角で車を止めて下さい。
[止める *tomeru*]

Please stop the car at that corner.

*Asoko ni atarashii mise ga narande iru.*

あそこに新しい店が並んでいる。

[並ぶ *narabu*]

There's a row of new shops there.

*Tēburu no ue ni, naifu to fōku o narabeta.*

テーブルの上に、ナイフとフォークを並べた。
[並べる *naraberu*]

I arranged the knives and forks on the table.

**Intransitive**

*Mado kara kaze ga haitte kuru.*

窓から風が入ってくる。

[入る *hairu*]

Wind blows in through the window.

**Transitive**

*Kono koppu ni jūsu o ire-mashō.*

このコップにジュースを入れましょう。

[入れる *ireru*]

Let's put some juice into these glasses.

# States of Being 状態を表す言い方

Intransitive Verb 自動詞

  *-te + iru*       ーて+いる

    *tsuite iru*     ついている [つく *tsuku*]

Transitive Verb 他動詞

  *-te + aru*      ーて+ある

    *tsukete aru*   つけてある [つける *tsukeru*]

The *-te* form can be used to describe an action whose results continue into the present. It is followed by *iru* いる (formal: *imasu* います) if the verb is intransitive and shows nothing more than a continuous state of being, and by *aru* ある (formal: *arimasu* あります) if the verb is transitive and shows purposeful action that has led to the present state of being.

## Intransitive Verb Examples

田中：山田さんの部屋の電気、ついていますね。[つく *tsuku*]

佐藤：窓もあいていますから、今晩は家にいるんでしょう。[開く *aku*]

*Tanaka: Yamada-san no heya no denki, tsuite imasu ne.*

*Satō: Mado mo aite imasu kara, komban wa ie ni iru n' deshō.*

Tanaka: The lights are on in Mr. Yamada's room.

Satō: The window is open, too. He must be at home this evening.

門の前に車が止まっています。[止まる *tomaru*]
*Mon no mae ni kuruma ga tomatte imasu.*
A car is parked in front of the gate.

## Transitive Verb Examples

もうすぐお客様が来ますから、部屋のクーラーも、電気もつけてあります。テーブルの上にはスプーンとフォークと皿が並べてあります。[つける *tsukeru*, 並べる *naraberu*]

*Mō sugu okyaku-sama ga kimasu kara, heya no kūrā mo, denki mo tsukete arimasu. Tēburu no ue ni wa supūn to fōku to sara ga narabete arimasu.*

Since guests will be coming soon, the air conditioner and the lights in the room have been switched on. And spoons, forks, and plates have been arranged on the table.

暑いから窓が開けてあります。
*Atsui kara mado ga akete arimasu.*
The window is open (has been left open) since it's so hot.

# The Passive Voice 受け身の表現

| | |
|---|---|
| ① /-~~nai~~/ + reru | ／－~~ない~~／＋れる |
|    ika/~~nai~~/reru | 行か／~~ない~~／れる |
| ② /-~~nai~~/ + rareru | ／－~~ない~~／＋られる |
|    mi/~~nai~~/rareru | 見／~~ない~~／られる |
| ③ kuru → korareru | 来る → 来られる |
|    suru → sareru | する → される |

The passive is formed as follows:

① Add *-reru* ーれる to the */-nai/* stem:
   ika/~~nai~~/reru    行か／~~ない~~／れる [行く *iku*]

② Add *-rareru* ーられる to the */-nai/* stem:
   tabe/~~nai~~/rareru  食べ／~~ない~~／られる [食べる *taberu*]

③　*kuru → korareru*　来る → 来られる
　　*suru → sareru*　する → される

Passive forms are conjugated as Group 2 verbs. For example, the *-masu* form of *ikareru* 行かれる is *ikaremasu* 行かれます.

## Sentence Structure

There are two types of passive sentences, direct and indirect. The direct type is very similar to the English passive, but the indirect passive has no direct English correlate.

### ■ Direct Passive

> Subject *wa* agent *ni* transitive verb in passive form

The basic structure of the direct passive is shown in the box above. (The "agent" is the one that carries out the action of the verb. In the English sentence "The man was bitten by the dog," the agent is "the dog.")

● Examples

私は社長に褒められました。 [褒める *homeru*]
*Watashi wa shachō ni homeraremashita.*
I was praised by the company president.

この本は若い女性によく読まれている。 [読む *yomu*]
*Kono hon wa wakai josei ni yoku yomarete iru.*
This book is read a lot by young women.

The direct passive is often used in expressions meaning "it is thought" or "it is said." The particle *to* と is used:

戦争が起きそうだと言われている。
*Sensō ga okisō da to iwarete iru.*
It is said that war is likely to break out.

### ■ Indirect Passive

The indirect passive conveys the notion that the subject of the sentence has suffered as a result of the action described by the verb. This use of the passive is very common in Japanese.

If the verb is transitive, the basic sentence structure is:

> Subject *wa* agent *ni* direct object *o* transitive verb in passive form

In English, passive verbs cannot take direct objects. In Japanese they can, as shown by the following examples.

福田：（私は）混んだ電車の中で財布を盗まれてしまって。[盗む *nusumu*]

岡山：それは大変だったね。駅員に言った？

*Fukuda: (Watashi wa) konda densha no naka de saifu o nusumarete shimatte.*

*Okayama: Sore wa taihen datta ne. Ekiin ni itta?*

Fukuda: I had my wallet stolen on a crowded train.

Okayama: That must have been terrible. Did you tell a station attendant?

（私は）犬に手をかまれた。[かむ *kamu*]

*(Watashi wa) inu ni te o kamareta.*

My hand was bitten by a dog.

（友達は）子供に時計を壊された。[壊す *kowasu*]

*(Tomodachi wa) kodomo ni tokei o kowasareta.*

A friend of mine had her watch broken by her child.

When the verb is intransitive, the basic sentence pattern for the indirect passive is:

> Subject + *wa* + agent + *ni* + intransitive verb in passive form

In English, intransitive verbs such as "to fall" or "to die" cannot be used in the passive. In Japanese they can:

乾：日曜日のゴルフどうだった？

嶋崎：せっかく行ったのに、雨に降られちゃったよ。[降る *furu*]

*Inui: Nichiyōbi no gorufu dō datta?*

*Shimazaki: Sekkaku itta no ni, ame ni furarechatta yo.*

Inui: How was golf on Sunday?

Shimazaki: We made a special effort to go, but we got rained on.

In the above example, *furarechatta* 降られちゃった is a contraction of *furarete shimatta* 降られてしまった (see page 94).

あの子は両親に死なれて、一人になった。[死ぬ *shinu*]
*Ano ko wa ryōshin ni shinarete, hitori ni natta.*
That child had his parents die on him, and now he's all alone.

# The Causative 使役の表現

| | |
|---|---|
| ① /-~~nai~~/ + seru | ／ー~~ない~~／＋せる |
|   *ika/~~nai~~/seru* | 行か／~~ない~~／せる |
| ② /-~~nai~~/ + saseru | ／ー~~ない~~／＋させる |
|   *mi/~~nai~~/saseru* | 見／~~ない~~／させる |
| ③ *kuru → kosaseru* | 来る → 来させる |
|   *suru → saseru* | する → させる |

The causative expresses the idea of making or causing somebody to do something. This form is derived as follows:

① Add *-seru* ーせる to the */-nai/* stem:
  *noma(~~nai~~)seru* 飲ま(~~ない~~)せる [飲む *nomu*]

② Add *-saseru* ーさせる to the */-nai/* stem:
  *tabe(~~nai~~)saseru* 食べ(~~ない~~)させる [食べる *taberu*]

③ *kuru → kosaseru* 来る → 来させる
  *suru → saseru* する → させる

Causative forms are conjugated as Group 2 verbs, so the *-masu* form of *nomaseru* 飲ませる is *nomasemasu* 飲ませます.

The following is a basic sentence pattern for causative verbs:

Subject *wa/ga* causee *o/ni* verb in causative form

## Formal Example

母親は子供を歩かせました。 [歩く *aruku*]
*Hahaoya wa kodomo o arukasemashita.*
The mother made the child walk.

## Informal Examples

父が弟を学校へ行かせた。 [行く *iku*]
*Chichi ga otōto o gakkō e ikaseta.*
My father had my younger brother go to school.

兄は妹を泣かせた。 [泣く *naku*]
*Ani wa imōto o nakaseta.*
My older brother made my little sister cry.

先生はその学生に歌わせた。[歌う *utau*]
*Sensei wa sono gakusei ni utawaseta.*
The teacher had that student sing.

With direct objects, the basic causative sentence pattern is:

Subject *wa/ga* causee *o/ni* direct object *o* verb in causative form

## Examples

先生は学生に作文を書かせた。 [書く *kaku*]
*Sensei wa gakusei ni sakubun o kakaseta.*
The teacher had the students write compositions.

母親は赤ちゃんにミルクを飲ませた。 [飲む *nomu*]
*Hahaoya wa akachan ni miruku o nomaseta.*
The mother fed milk to her baby.

社長は秘書に手紙を出させた。 [出す *dasu*]
*Shachō wa hisho ni tegami o dasaseta.*
The president had his secretary send the letter.

父は子供を買物に行かせた。[行く *iku*]
*Chichi wa kodomo o kaimono ni ikaseta.*
The father sent his child shopping.

# The Causative–Passive 使役受身の表現 （人に何かさせられたときの言い方）

Causative verbs can be made into passive verbs, thus forming what are called causative-passive verbs. The passive suffix *-rareru* －られる is added to the causative verb's */-nai/* stem.

| Causative /-~~nai~~/ + *rareru* | 使役 ／－~~ない~~／ ＋ られる |
|---|---|
| ① *nomase(~~nai~~)rareru* | 飲ませ(~~ない~~)られる<br>[飲む *nomu*] |
| ② *tabesase(~~nai~~)rareru* | 食べさせ(~~ない~~)られる<br>[食べる *taberu*] |
| ③ *kosase(~~nai~~)rareru* | 来させ(~~ない~~)られる<br>[来る *kuru*] |
| *sase(~~nai~~)rareru* | させ(~~ない~~)られる [する *suru*] |

Some Group 1 verbs have special causative-passive forms in addition to their regular one:

*ikaserareru* → *ikasareru*　　行かせられる → 行かされる
　　　　　　　　　　　　　　[行く *iku*]
*mataserareru* → *matasareru*　待たせられる → 待たされる
　　　　　　　　　　　　　　[待つ *matsu*]

Though sometimes difficult to render into English, the meaning of the causative-passive is roughly "to be forced to have something done to one" or "to have to do something although one would prefer not to."

## Examples

友達に一時間も待たされました（待たせられました）。
[待つ *matsu*]
*Tomodachi ni ichijikan mo matasaremashita (mataser-aremashita).*
I was made to wait a full hour by my friend.

清水：顔色が悪いね。

泉：きのうの晩、課長に酒を飲まされて今日は調子が悪いんだ。[飲む *nomu*]

*Shimizu: Kaoiro ga warui ne.*

*Izumi: Kinō no ban, kachō ni sake o nomasarete kyō wa chōshi ga warui n' da.*

Shimizu: You're looking pretty bad.

Izumi: Last night I was made to drink saké by the section chief. Today I'm in bad shape.

久米：明日は結婚式なんだって。

松村：そうなんだよ。祝辞を述べさせられるんで、いやだね。[述べる *noberu*]

*Kume: Ashita wa kekkon-shiki nan datte.*

*Matsumura: Sō nan da yo. Shukuji o nobesaserareru n' de, iya da ne.*

Kume: I hear that you're going to a wedding tomorrow.

Matsumura: That's right. I'm being forced to give a speech. What a pain.

きのうは会社に９時までいさせられた。[いる *iru*]

*Kinō wa kaisha ni kuji made isaserareta.*

Yesterday I was forced to be in the office until nine o'clock.

母に朝早くから、掃除をさせられた。[する *suru*]

*Haha ni asa hayaku kara, sōji o saserareta.*

I was forced by my mother to clean house beginning early in the morning.

社長に駅まで迎えに来させられた。[来る *kuru*]

*Shachō ni eki made mukae ni kosaserareta.*

I was ordered by the company president to come meet him at the station.

# Giving Advice and Making Suggestions
## 忠告や提案を表す言い方

(1) -te + wa ikaga deshō ka　ーて＋はいかがでしょうか

　 *mite wa ikaga deshō ka*　見てはいかがでしょうか

| | |
|---|---|
| *-te + wa ikaga desu ka* | ーて＋はいかがですか |
| *mite wa ikaga desu ka* | 見てはいかがですか |
| *-te + wa dō deshō ka* | ーて＋はどうでしょうか |
| *mite wa dō deshō ka* | 見てはどうでしょうか |
| *-te + wa dō desu ka* | ーて＋はどうですか |
| *mite wa dō desu ka* | 見てはどうですか |
| (2) *-ta + hō ga ii desu* | ーた＋ほうがいいです |
| *mita hō ga ii desu* | 見たほうがいいです |
| *-ta + hō ga ii* | ーた＋ほうがいい |
| *mita hō ga ii* | 見たほうがいい |

## (1) *Ikaga* いかが and *dō* どう

One way to say make a polite suggestion is with the *-te* form followed by *wa* は, which in turn is followed by either *ikaga* いかが or *dō* どう "how" and then either *deshō ka* でしょうか or *desu ka* ですか. Here are the four possible patterns in descending order of politeness:

| | |
|---|---|
| *-te wa ikaga deshō ka* | ーてはいかがでしょうか |
| *-te wa ikaga desu ka* | ーてはいかがですか |
| *-te wa dō deshō ka* | ーてはどうでしょうか |
| *-te wa dō desu ka* | ーてはどうですか |

In essence, they all mean, "How about doing...?"

■ **Examples**

課長：この手紙速達で送ってくれないか。
中野：ファックスを送ってはいかがでしょうか。[送る *okuru*]

*Kachō: Kono tegami sokutatsu de okutte kurenai ka.*
*Nakano: Fakkusu o okutte wa ikaga deshō ka.*

Section chief: Could you send this letter by express mail for me?
Nakano: How about sending a fax?

すぐいらしてはいかがですか。[いらっしゃる *irassharu*, polite form of 行く *iku*]

*Sugu irashite wa ikaga desu ka.*
Would you care to go soon?

あれを買ってはどうですか。 [買う *kau*]
*Are o katte wa dō desu ka.*
How about buying that one?

## (2) *Hō ga ii* ほうがいい

To make suggestions more directly, use the informal past tense (*-ta*) form followed by *hō ga ii desu* ほうがいいです (formal) or *hō ga ii* ほうがいい (informal).

> ... *shita hō ga ii*      〜したほうがいい
> You should ...

### ■Example

恵子：風邪かしら、頭が痛いの。
信子：それなら早く休んだほうがいいわ。 [休む *yasumu*]
*Keiko: Kaze kashira, atama ga itai no.*
*Nobuko: Sore nara hayaku yasunda hō ga ii wa.*
Keiko: I wonder if I have a cold. My head hurts.
Nobuko: In that case, you should rest right away.

## Expressing Time Relationships 時を表す言い方

Japanese has many ways to describe how one action precedes or follows another in time. The following sections explain "before," "after," "about to do," continuing and completed actions, and doing something in advance.

## Before 一つの動作の前に何かをする言い方

| | |
|---|---|
| plain form + *mae ni* | 原形 + 前に |
| *iku mae ni* | 行く前に |
| before going | |

Use the plain form of the verb followed by *mae ni* 前に:

飛行機に乗る前に、荷物の手続きをしなければならない。

*Hikōki ni noru mae ni, nimotsu no tetsuzuki o shina-kereba naranai.*

Before boarding the airplane, you must go through the baggage procedures.

毎晩寝る前に本を読む。
*Maiban neru mae ni hon o yomu.*
I read books every night before going to sleep.

## After 一つの動作のあとに何かをする言い方 ━━━━

| | |
|---|---|
| (1) *-te + kara* | ーて＋から |
| *itte kara* | 行ってから |
| (2) *-ta + ato (de)* | ーた＋後(で) |
| *itta ato (de)* | 行ったあと（で） |
| (3) *-ta + totan* | ーた＋とたん |
| *itta totan* | 行ったとたん |

### ■(1) *-Te kara* ーてから

One way to say that one action follows another is to use the *-te* form followed by *kara* から. It usually indicates that one action follows closely on another.

*tabete kara*　　　　食べてから
after eating

● Examples

食事をしてから出かけよう。 [する *suru*]
*Shokuji o shite kara dekakeyō.*
Let's leave after we have a meal.

家へ帰ってからゆっくりテレビを見た。 [帰る *kaeru*]
*Ie e kaette kara yukkuri terebi o mita.*
After returning home, I relaxed and watched some television.

### ■(2) *-Ta ato (de)* ーた後 (で)

Another pattern for "after" is the informal past tense (*-ta*) form followed by *ato* 後 or *ato de* 後で. In this case, the one action does not necessarily follow closely upon the other.

*tabeta ato*　　　　　　　食べた後
after eating

● Examples

私達が出かけた後で、谷さんが来たらしい。[出かける *dekakeru*]
*Watashi-tachi ga dekaketa ato de, Tani-san ga kita rashii.*
It seems that Mr. Tani came by after we had left home.

食事をした後、映画を見た。[する *suru*]
*Shokuji o shita ato, eiga o mita.*
After I ate, I saw a movie.

■ **(3) *-Ta totan* ーたとたん**

This expression means "immediately after" and is often used with sudden, unexpected actions. It consists of the *-ta* form followed by *totan* とたん.

飛行機が着陸したとたん、火を吹いた。[する *suru*]
*Hikōki ga chakuriku shita totan, hi o fuita.*
The instant the airplane touched ground, it caught on fire.

ホテルに着いたとたん、雨が降り出した。[着く *tsuku*]
*Hoteru ni tsuita totan, ame ga furidashita.*
As soon as we reached the hotel, it started raining.

## About to Do Something　動作が行なわれる直前の言い方

| | |
|---|---|
| (1) ① /-~~ru~~/ + *ō* + *to suru* | |
| ik/~~u~~/*ō to suru* | 行こうとする |
| ② /-~~ru~~/ + *yō* + *to suru* | ／ー~~る~~／ + よう + とする |
| mi/~~ru~~/*yō to suru* | 見／~~る~~／ようとする |
| ③ *kuru* → *koyō to suru* | 来る → 来ようとする |
| *suru* → *shiyō to suru* | する → しようとする |
| (2) plain form + *tokoro* | 原形 + ところ |

| *yomu tokoro* | 読むところ |
| (3) plain form + *bakari* | 原形 + ばかり |
| *taberu bakari* | 食べるばかり |

There are several strategies for saying that one is about to do something.

### ■(1) *to suru* とする

The informal volitional form is followed by *to suru* とする. This pattern often describes an action that is halted just before it can begin.

*ikō to suru*　　　　　行こうとする [行く *iku*]
to be about to go

*tabeyō to suru*　　　　食べようとする [食べる *taberu*]
to be about to eat

● Examples

お風呂に入ろうとすると、電話が鳴った。 [入る *hairō*]
*O-furo ni hairō to suru to, denwa ga natta.*
Just when I was about to get in the bath, the phone rang.

いま選手はプールに飛び込もうとしています。 [飛び込む *tobikomu*]
*Ima senshu wa pūru ni tobikomō to shite imasu.*
The swimmers are just about to dive into the pool.

テレビを見ようとしたら、停電になった。 [見る *miru*]
*Terebi o miyō to shitara, teiden ni natta.*
We were about to watch television when the electricity went out.

### ■(2) *tokoro* ところ

This pattern expresses the sense of being on the verge of doing something. The plain form of the verb is followed by *tokoro da* ところだ (informal) or *tokoro desu* ところです (formal). It differs from the *to suru* pattern in that the former shows intention while this pattern doesn't.

*kuru tokoro da*      来るところだ
to be about to come

● Examples

父はいま出かけるところです。
*Chichi wa ima dekakeru tokoro desu.*
My dad is just about to leave.

映画が始まるところですよ。
*Eiga ga hajimaru tokoro desu yo.*
The movie is going to begin any minute.

■ **(3) *bakari da*** ばかりだ

In this case, the plain form of the verb is followed by *bakari da* ばかりだ (informal) or *bakari desu* ばかりです (formal). This pattern says only that all preparations for the action of the verb have been completed. It does not necessarily mean that the action will take place soon.

*dekakeru bakari da*      出かけるばかりだ
to have nothing left to do but to leave

● Examples

もう出かけるばかりですよ。
*Mō dekakeru bakari desu yo.*
We're ready to leave now.

食事の用意もすっかりできました。あとは食べるばかりです。
*Shokuji no yōi mo sukkari dekimashita. Ato wa taberu bakari desu.*
I've wrapped up all the preparations for the meal. All we have to do is eat.

## Continuing Actions 動作が進行中 ━━━━━

| | |
|---|---|
| *-te + iru tokoro da* | ―て + いるところだ |
|   *nonde iru tokoro da* | 飲んでいるところだ [飲む *nomu*] |
| to be drinking | |

As described on page 25, one technique for describing continuing actions is to use the present progressive (*-te + iru*). The immediacy of the action can be emphasized by following *-te iru* with *tokoro da* ところだ (informal) or *tokoro desu* ところです (formal).

## ■Examples

赤ん坊は眠っているところなんです。 [眠る *nemuru*]
*Akambō wa nemutte iru tokoro nan desu.*
The baby is sleeping at the moment.

姉はいまケーキを焼いているところです。 [焼く *yaku*]
*Ane wa ima kēki o yaite iru tokoro desu.*
My older sister is baking a cake right now.

## Completed Actions 動作の完了を表す言い方 ——

| | |
|---|---|
| (1) *-ta + tokoro da* | ーた＋ところだ |
|     *owatta todoro da* | 終わったところだ |
|     to have just finished | |
| (2) *-te + shimatta* | ーて＋しまった |
|     *nete shimatta* | 寝てしまった |
|     to have just fallen asleep | |
| (3) *-ta + bakari da* | ーた＋ばかりだ |
|     *kaetta bakari da* | 帰ったばかりだ |
|     to have just returned | |

## ■(1) *tokoro da* ところだ

When the informal past tense (*-ta*) form is used before *tokoro da* ところだ or *tokoro desu* ところです, it means that the action has just been completed.

    *yomiowatta tokoro da*    読み終わったところだ
                                   [読み終わる *yomiowaru*]

    to have just finished reading

● Examples

山田さんは今会社を出たところです。 [出る *deru*]
*Yamada-san wa ima kaisha o deta tokoro desu.*
Ms. Yamada has just left the office.

弟はたった今帰ったところだ。 [帰る *kaeru*]
*Otōto wa tattaima kaetta tokoro da.*
My younger brother returned home just a moment ago.

■ **(2)** *shimatta* しまった

The Group 1 verb *shimau* しまう is used as an auxiliary after the *-te* form to indicate primarily that an action is completely finished; secondarily, it can indicate regret for the action specified by the preceding verb.

*tabete shimatta* 　　　　食べてしまった [食べる *taberu*]
to have eaten completely; to have regrettably eaten

● Examples

必要な書類はみんなタイプしてしまいました。[する *suru*]
*Hitsuyō na shorui wa minna taipu shite shimaimashita.*
I've finished typing all the necessary documents.

作文の宿題を書いてしまった。 [書く *kaku*]
*Sakubun no shukudai o kaite shimatta.*
I finished writing the homework composition.

きのうまた飲み過ぎてしまった。
*Kinō mata nomisugite shimatta.*
I went and drank too much again yesterday.

■ **Note**

The *-te shimau* form is often contracted in colloquial speech to *-chau* ーちゃう (present tense) or *-chatta* ーちゃった (past tense).

*shite shimau* → *shichau* 　　　してしまう → しちゃう
　　　　　　　　　　　　　　　　　[する *suru*]
*shite shimatta* → *shichatta* 　してしまった → しちゃった

● Examples

アイスクリーム、みんな溶けちゃった。[溶ける *tokeru*]
*Aisukurīmu, minna tokechatta.*
All the ice cream melted.

その仕事は全部やっちゃったよ。[やる *yaru*]
*Sono shigoto wa zembu yatchatta yo.*
I finished off all that work.

■ **(3)** *bakari* ばかり

Another way to say that an action has just been completed is to use the informal past tense (*-ta*) followed by *bakari da* ばかりだ or *bakari desu* ばかりです.

 *kaita bakari da*     書いたばかりだ [書く *kaku*]
 to have just finished writing

● Examples

田中さんと昼ご飯を食べたばかりなんです。[食べる *taberu*]
*Tanaka-san to hiru-gohan o tabeta bakari nan desu.*
I just ate lunch with Mr. Tanaka.

テレビでそのニュースが放映されたばかりだ。[する *suru*]
*Terebi de sono nyūsu ga hōei sareta bakari da.*
That news was just broadcast on television.

## Doing Something in Advance 準備や保存のために 前もって何かをする言い方

| | |
|---|---|
| *-te + oku* | ーて + おく |
|  *tsukutte oku* | 作っておく [作る *tsukuru*] |
|  to make something (for later use) | |
|  *shite oku* | しておく [する *suru*] |
|  to do something (in advance) | |

When the *-te* form is followed by the verb *oku* おく, the meaning is to do something in advance or as preparation for something else; it can also mean to put away or preserve for later use.

■ **Examples**

お客さんが来ますから、テーブルの上にコーヒーカップを並べておいて下さい。[並べる *naraberu*]

*O-kyaku-san ga kimasu kara, tēburu no ue ni kōhī kappu o narabete oite kudasai.*

Customers will be coming, so put out the coffee cups on the tables beforehand.

夏の洋服は箱にしまっておきます。[しまう *shimau*]

*Natsu no yōfuku wa hako ni shimatte okimasu.*

I put my summer clothes away in a box (until next summer).

ケーキを作って、冷蔵庫に入れておいた。[入れる *ireru*]

*Kēki o tsukutte, reizōko ni irete oita.*

I made a cake and put it in the refrigerator (to be eaten later on).

明日は試験だから、今晩は勉強をしておかなくっちゃ。[する *suru*]

*Ashita wa shiken da kara, komban wa benkyō o shite okanakutcha.*

There's a test tomorrow, so I have to study tonight.

## Giving a Reason 理由を表す言い方

| *-te* ーて | |
|---|---|
| *mite* | 見て |

The *-te* form often explains the reason for the action in the clause that follows.

長い時間テレビを見て、目が痛くなりました。[見る *miru*]

*Nagai jikan terebi o mite, me ga itaku narimashita.*

I watched television for a long time, so my eyes started to hurt.

雨が降って、ゴルフに行けなかった。[降る *furu*]
*Ame ga futte, gorufu ni ikenakatta.*
It was raining, so I couldn't go golfing.

Note that this form cannot be followed by commands, suggestions, or statements of intent.

---

# Expressing Regret 後悔や残念な気持を表す言い方

---

| (1) *-te + shimau* | ー て + しまう |
| --- | --- |
| *ochite shimau* | 落ちてしまう [落ちる to fall] |
| (2) /-~nai~/ + *nakereba* | ／ー~なー~／ + なければ |
| *yokatta* | よかった |
| *noma*/~nai~/*nakereba* | 飲ま／~なー~／なければ |
| *yokatta* | よかった |

---

## (1) *-te shimau* ー てしまう ━━━━━━━━

The *-te* form followed by *shimau* しまう is used to express regret over something one has done. (This is different from the sense of completed action described on page 94 for the *-te shimau* form.)

### ■ Examples

また朝寝坊をしてしまった。[する *suru*]
*Mata asa nebō o shite shimatta.*
I slept late again.

うっかり居眠りをして、事故を起こしてしまった。[起こす *okosu*]
*Ukkari inemuri o shite, jiko o okoshite shimatta.*
I fell asleep without realizing it and caused an accident.

## (2) -nakereba yokatta －なければよかった ━━━━━━

A more explicit expression of regret can be made by attaching *nakereba yokatta* なければよかった to the */-nai/* stem.

*Noma/~~nai~~/nakereba yokatta.*　飲ま／~~ない~~／なければよかった。

It would have been better if I hadn't drunk that.

### ■ Examples

こんなセーター、買わなければよかった。 [買う *kau*]
*Konna sētā, kawanakereba yokatta.*
I wish I hadn't bought this sweater.

いま思えば、この会社に入らなければよかったのかもしれない。 [入る *hairu*]
*Ima omoeba, kono kaisha ni hairanakereba yokatta no kamo shirenai.*
Now that I think about it, maybe it would have been better if I hadn't joined this company.

# Expressing Conjecture 推量を表す言い方

(1) Based on Direct Knowledge
　　plain form + *yō da*　　　　原形 + ようだ
　　*furu yō da* (to rain)　　　　降るようだ

(2) Based on Hearsay
　　plain form + *rashii*　　　　原形 + らしい
　　*furu rashii*　　　　　　　　降るらしい

(3) Based on Supposition or Guess
　　plain form + *darō*　　　　　原形 + だろう
　　*furu darō*　　　　　　　　　降るだろう

(4) Based on Reasonable Conviction
　　plain form + *hazu da*　　　　原形 + はずだ
　　*kuru hazu da*　　　　　　　来るはずだ

There are several strategies for expressing conjecture or supposition. The choice depends on the source and certainty of the information.

## (1) *yō da* ようだ

If you believe that something is probably true based on your own experience or knowledge, you can use the plain form followed by *yō da* ようだ (informal) or *yō desu* ようです (formal).

*kuru yō da*          来るようだ
to be likely to come [will apparently come]

■ **Examples**

社長は来週アメリカへ行くようだ。
*Shachō wa raishū Amerika e iku yō da.*
It seems that the president is going to the U.S. next week.

来週内閣が解散するようだ。
*Raishū naikaku ga kaisan suru yō da.*
The cabinet is probably going to be dissolved next week.

## (2) *rashii* らしい

To mention something that you suppose to be true because you have heard it or read it, use the plain form followed by *rashii* らしい:

*iku rashii*          行くらしい
to be thought to be going

■ **Examples**

次の試験は来週あるらしい。
*Tsugi no shiken wa raishū aru rashii.*
Apparently the next test will be next week.

天気予報によると、今晩から台風の影響で海が荒れるらしい。
*Tenki yohō ni yoru to, konban kara taifū no eikyō de umi ga areru rashii.*
According to the weather report, the sea should get choppy

tonight because of the effect of the typhoon.

## (3) *darō* だろう

To say what you think or guess, use the plain form with *darō* だろう (informal) or *deshō* でしょう (formal). These are the volitional forms of the copula *da* だ. After *darō* だろう you can also use *to omou* と思う (formal: *to omoimasu* と思います) "I think."

> *Furu darō.*            降るだろう。
> It will probably rain.

### ■ Examples

明日のパーティに彼は来ないだろう。 [来る *kuru*]
*Ashita no pāti ni kare wa konai darō.*
He is not likely to come to tomorrow's party.

今度の交渉はうまく行くだろうと思うんですが。
*Kondo no kōshō wa umaku iku darō to omou n' desu ga.*
I think that the negotiations should go smoothly this time.

## (4) *hazu da* はずだ

If you think that what you say must be true, use the plain form followed by *hazu da* はずだ (informal) or *hazu desu* はずです (formal).

> *iku hazu*            行くはず
> to be expected to go

### ■ Examples

本田：谷さんから電話こないんだけど、どうしたのかしら。
小泉：くるはずですよ。きのう会った時、必ず電話するって言ってましたから。

*Honda (female): Tani-san kara denwa konai n' da kedo, dō shita no kashira.*

*Koizumi: Kuru hazu desu yo. Kinō atta toki, kanarazu denwa suru 'tte yutte 'mashita kara.*

Honda: There's still no telephone call from Mr. Tani. I wonder what's happened.

Koizumi: I expect the call to come. When I saw him yesterday, he said that he would be sure to call.

課長はそれを知っているはずです。
*Kachō wa sore o shitte iru hazu desu.*
The section chief should know that.

## Conjecture about the Past

If you are expressing a conjecture about something that may have happened in the past, you can replace the plain form with the informal past tense (*-ta*) form in any of the above four patterns. Here's an example with *yō* よう:

道が濡れているから、夕べは雨が降ったようだ。[降る *furu*]
*Michi ga nurete iru kara, yūbe wa ame ga futta yō da.*
The street is wet. I guess it must have rained last night.

# Reporting Something Heard or Experienced
伝聞や状態の言い方

(1) Reporting Something Heard
    plain form + *sō da*        原形 + そうだ
     *yomu sō da*          読むそうだ
(2) Reporting Something Experienced
    /-~~masu~~/ + *sō da*      ／－~~ます~~／＋そうだ
    *furi/~~masu~~/sō da*     降り／~~ます~~／そうだ

## (1) Reporting Something Heard

To report something that you have heard, use the plain form followed by *sō da* そうだ (informal) or *sō desu* そうです (formal):

*Furu sō desu.*        降るそうです。
I hear it's going to rain.

### ■ Examples

In the following examples, the そうだ *sō da* is not translated into English because the "According to ..." expresses the same meaning.

テレビのニュースによると、台風が来るそうだ。

*Terebi no nyūsu ni yoru to, taifū ga kuru sō da.*

According to the TV news, a typhoon is coming.

部長の話だと、あの会社の経営は近ごろうまく行っていないそうだ。 [行く *iku*]

*Buchō no hanashi da to, ano kaisha no keiei wa chika-goro umaku itte inai sō da.*

According to what the department chief says, that company's operations haven't been going very well lately.

## (2) Reporting Something Seen

To report something that you have seen or otherwise experienced, use the /-*masu*/ stem before *sō da* そうだ (informal) or *sō desu* そうです (formal).

*Furi/~~masu~~/sō da.*    降り／~~ます~~／そうだ。[降る *furu*]

It looks like it's going to rain.

### ■ Examples

雨が降ってきそうですね。 [くる *kuru*]

*Ame ga futte kisō desu ne.*

It looks like it's going to start raining.

あの選手は疲れきっていて、今にも倒れそうじゃないですか。 [倒れる *taoreru*]

*Ano senshu wa tsukarekitte ite, ima ni mo taoresō ja nai desu ka.*

That athlete is worn out. Doesn't she look as though she's going to collapse at any moment?

# 3

# Verb Endings

Many verb compounds can be formed by appending one verb to the end of another. In most cases, the second verb is attached to the */-masu/* stem of the first verb. For example, the *-masu* form of *furu* 降る is *furimasu* 降ります, so the */-masu/* stem is *furi* 降り. When this stem is combined with the ending *dasu* 出す as in the first pattern shown below, the verb compound *furidasu* 降り出す is formed.

In some compounds, the first verb takes the *-te* form instead of the */-masu/* stem. Examples of this type begin on page 116.

## Start of Action 動作の始まり ━━━━━━━

| | |
|---|---|
| (1) /-~~masu~~/ + *dasu* | ／－~~ま す~~／ + 出す |
| *furi/~~masu~~/dasu* | 降り／~~ま す~~／出す |
| (2) /-~~masu~~/ + *hajimeru* | ／－~~ま す~~／ + 始める |
| *hashiri/~~masu~~/hajimeru* | 走り／~~ま す~~／始める |

The endings *dasu* 出す and *hajimeru* 始める indicate the start of an action, with the former generally indicating a greater burst of energy: compare *hashirihajimeru* 走り始める (to start running) and *hashiridasu* 走り出す (to dash forth). They are attached only to verbs that describe continuous actions. As a suffix, *-dasu* has additional meanings that have to do with sending something forth or causing something to appear, as in *mitsukedasu* 見つけ出す (to find out) and *omoidasu* 思い出す (to recall).

(1)夜になって、雪が降り出した。[降る *furu*]

*Yoru ni natte, yuki ga furidashita.*

When night came, snow began to fall.

そのロックコンサートの切符は一日から売り出すそうだ。
[売る *uru*]

*Sono rokku konsāto no kippu wa tsuitachi kara uridasu
sō da.*

I've heard that they're going to start selling the tickets for
that rock concert on the first of the month.

(2)雨が降り始めた。

*Ame ga furihajimeta.*

It has started to rain.

信号が変わると、待っていた車がそろって走り始めた。
[走る *hashiru*]

*Shingō ga kawaru to, matte ita kuruma ga sorotte hashiri-
hajimeta.*

When the signal changed, the waiting cars started moving
en masse.

## Half-Completed Action 動作が中途である状態 ━━━

| | |
|---|---|
| /-~~masu~~/ + *kakeru* | ／ー~~ます~~／ + かける |
| *yomi*/~~masu~~/*kakeru* | 読み／~~ます~~／かける |

The ending *kakeru* かける indicates that an action has
been started but has not been brought to a finish or end.

手紙を書きかけたんですが、まだ書いていません。[書く
*kaku*]

*Tegami o kakikaketa n' desu ga, mada kaite imasen.*

I got started on the letter, but I haven't finished writing it yet.

きのうは疲れていて、本を読みかけたまま眠ってしまっ
た。[読む *yomu*]

*Kinō wa tsukarete ite, hon o yomikaketa mama nemutte
shimatta.*

I was so tired yesterday, I fell asleep in the middle of
reading a book.

## Continuation of Action 動作の継続 ━━━━━

| | |
|---|---|
| (1) /-~~masu~~/ + tsuzuku | ／－~~ます~~／＋続く |
| furi/~~masu~~/tsuzuku | 降り／~~ます~~／続く |
| (2) /-~~masu~~/ + tsuzukeru | ／－~~ます~~／＋続ける |
| utai/~~masu~~/tsuzukeru | 歌い／~~ます~~／続ける |

The intransitive ending *tsuzuku* 続く and its transitive counterpart *tsuzukeru* 続ける indicate that the action is continuing.

(1) 雨が何日も降り続いている。 [降る *furu*]
*Ame ga nannichi mo furitsuzuite iru.*
The rain hasn't let up for many days now.

(2) 彼女はもう5時間もピアノを弾き続けている。[弾く *hiku*]
*Kanojo wa mō gojikan mo piano o hikitsuzukete iru.*
She has been playing the piano for five hours without a break.

## End of an Action 動作の終了 ━━━━━

| | |
|---|---|
| (1) /-~~masu~~/ + owaru | －／~~ます~~／＋終わる |
| yomi/~~masu~~/owaru | 読み／~~ます~~／終わる |
| (2) /-~~masu~~/ + oeru | －／~~ます~~／＋終える |
| yomi/~~masu~~/oeru | 読み／~~ます~~／終える |
| (3) /-~~masu~~/ + agaru | ／－~~ます~~／＋上がる |
| deki/~~masu~~/agaru | でき／~~ます~~／上がる |
| (4) /-~~masu~~/ + ageru | ／－~~ます~~／＋上げる |
| kaki/~~masu~~/ageru | 書き／~~ます~~／上げる |

Notes: Transitive and intransitive verbs both appear in this category, so attention must be paid to the use of objects and particles.

These endings indicate that an action is completed. The first two are primarily confined to that meaning, while the latter have other meanings (which are not dealt with here) depending on what verb they are combined with.

(1) この手紙を書き終ったら、出かけます。 [書く *kaku*]
*Kono tegami o kakiowattara, dekakemasu.*
I'll leave after I finish writing this letter.

その仕事をし終えるのはいつごろですか。 [する *suru*]
*Sono shigoto o shioeru no wa itsu goro desu ka.*
When will you finish that work?

(2) この本を一ヶ月かけてやっと読み終えた。 [読み *yomi*]
*Kono hon o ikkagetsu kakete yatto yomioeta.*
After spending a month on this book, I was finally able to finish reading it.

歌手がその長い歌を歌い終えた時、聴衆はいっせいに立って拍手をした。 [歌う *utau*]
*Kashu ga sono nagai uta o utaioeta toki, chōshū wa issei ni tatte hakushu o shita.*
When the singer finished singing the long song, the audience rose in a body and applauded.

## Thoroughness of Action 動作の完成 ━━━━

| | |
|---|---|
| (1) /-~~masu~~/ + *kiru* | ／一~~ます~~／ ＋きる |
| *nomi*/~~masu~~/*kiru* | 飲み／~~ます~~／きる |
| (2) /-~~masu~~/ + *tōsu* | ／一~~ます~~／ ＋通す |
| *yomi*/~~masu~~/*tōsu* | 読み／~~ます~~／通す |
| (3) /-~~masu~~/ + *nuku* | ／一~~ます~~／ ＋ぬく |
| *yari*/~~masu~~/*nuku* | やり／~~ます~~／ぬく |

These endings indicate that an action has been done thoroughly and completely. Whereas *-kiru* indicates solely that an action has been done to completion or to the utmost extent, *-tōsu* and *-nuku* include the notion of doing something from beginning to end and imply that this was done in spite of adverse conditions. The latter two are often used interchangeably, although *-tōsu* places slightly more emphasis on the process of the action whereas *-nuku* 一抜く emphasizes the successful emergence from the process.

Here are some common verbs that incorporate these suffixes:

(1) *dashikiru*　　　　　　　　出し切る
    to give all one has (e.g., energy or money)

    *kashikiru*　　　　　　　　貸し切る
    to rent out completely (exclusively)

    *karikiru*　　　　　　　　借り切る
    to rent completely (exclusively)

    *kawakikiru*　　　　　　　乾き切る
    to dry out completely

    *moekiru*　　　　　　　　　燃え切る
    to burn up completely

    *noborikiru*　　　　　　　登り切る
    to climb completely (to the top)

    *yomikiru*　　　　　　　　読み切る
    to read completely (to the end)

    *nomikiru*　　　　　　　　飲み切る
    to drink all

(2) *arukitōsu*　　　　　　　歩き通す
    to walk all the way

    *hikitōsu*　　　　　　　　弾き通す
    to play (on a stringed instrument or piano) an entire piece

    *iitōsu*　　　　　　　　　言い通す
    to keeping saying the same thing throughout a process

    *kitōsu*　　　　　　　　　着通す
    to keep wearing (certain clothing throughout a certain period)

    *hatarakitōsu*　　　　　　働き通す
    to keep working throughout a certain period

*yaritōsu* (largely inter-　　　　やり通す
changeable with やり抜く)
to do (carry out) to the very end

*yomitōsu*　　　　　　　　　読み通す
to read all the way through

(3) *kakinuku*　　　　　　　　書き抜く
to finish writing (something particularly difficult)

*hashirinuku*　　　　　　　走り抜く
to complete a hard (running) race

*nebarinuku*　　　　　　　ねばり抜く
to continue from beginning to end without giving up

*semenuku*　　　　　　　　攻め抜く
to carry out a successful attack

*shirinuku*　　　　　　　　知り抜く
to know everything about

*yarinuku*　　　　　　　　やり抜く
to carry out to the end

Here are the suffixes used in complete sentences:

(1) 一日中働いて、疲れきった。[疲れる *tsukareru*]
*Ichinichi-jū hataraite, tsukarekitta.*
I worked all day long, and now I'm all worn out.

バスを１台借り切って、一泊旅行に出かけた。[借りる
*kariru*]
*Basu o ichidai karikitte, ippaku-ryokō ni dekaketa.*
We rented a bus all to ourselves and went off on a one-
night trip.

(2) 田中さんはとうとうその仕事をやり通した。[やる *yaru*]
*Tanaka-san wa tōtō sono shigoto o yaritōshita.*
Ms. Tanaka finally got through with all that work.

朝までかかって、その長い小説を読み通した。[読む
*yomu*]
*Asa made kakatte, sono nagai shōsetsu o yomitōshita.*
It took until morning, but I read that long novel through
to the end.

(3)佐藤：田中さん、とうとうあの仕事をやりぬいたそうで
　　すね。
　　山田：なかなか根性のある人ですね。

*Satō: Tanaka-san, tōtō ano shigoto o yarinuita sō desu
ne.*

*Yamada: Nakanaka konjō no aru hito desu ne.*

Satō: I heard that Ms. Tanaka finally finished all that
work.

Yamada: She's really gutsy, isn't she?

## Incomplete or Failed Action　動作が不完全だったり 失敗した状態 ━━━━

| | | | |
|---|---|---|---|
| (1) | /-~~masu~~/ + *wasureru* | ／－~~ます~~／ + 忘れる | |
| | *ii/~~masu~~/wasureru* | 言い／~~ます~~／忘れる | |
| (2) | /-~~masu~~/ + *otosu* | ／－~~ます~~／ + 落す | |
| | *kaki/~~masu~~/otosu* | 書き／~~ます~~／落す | |
| (3) | /-~~masu~~/ + *machigaeru* | ／－~~ます~~／ + 間違がえる | |
| | *mi/~~masu~~/machigaeru* | 見／~~ます~~／間違える | |
| | /-~~masu~~/ + *chigaeru* | ／－~~ます~~／ + 違がえる | |
| | *mi/~~masu~~/chigaeru* | 見／~~ます~~／違がえる | |

The ending *wasureru* 忘れる indicates that an action has
been forgotten, *otosu* 落す shows that the action was unin-
tentionally omitted, and *machigaeru* 間違がえる and *chi-
gaeru* 違がえる mean that a mistake was made and are
largely interchangeable in that sense. Some common verbs
incorporating these suffixes are:

(1)*(tegami o) dashiwasureru*　　　　（手紙を）出し忘れる
　　to forget to send (a letter)

　　*(denwa o) kakewasureru*　　　　（電話を）かけ忘れる
　　to forget to place (a telephone call)

　　*kaiwasureru*　　　　　　　　　　買い忘れる
　　to forget to buy

*okiwasureru* 置き忘れる
to forget to place something somewhere

*shimaiwasureru* しまい忘れる
to forget to put away

*shimewasureru* 閉め忘れる
to forget to close

*shiwasureru* し忘れる
to forget to do

(2) *kikiotosu* 聞き落とす
to fail to hear

*kaiotosu* 買い落とす
to fail to buy

*miotosu* 見落とす
to fail to see

*tsukeotosu* つけ落とす
to fail to attach

*yomiotosu* 読み落とす
to fail to read

(3) *kakichigaeru* 書き違える
to miswrite

*kakechigaeru* かけ違える
to mis-hang

*kazoechigaeru* 数え違える
to miscount

*norichigaeru* 乗り違える
to take the wrong (train etc.)

*nomichigaeru* 飲み違える
to drink the wrong (medicine etc.)

*omoichigaeru* 思い違える
to mistake (one thing for another in one's mind)

*torichigaeru* 取り違える
to take the wrong thing; to mis-take

| | |
|---|---|
| *yobichigaeru*<br>to miscall | 呼び違える |
| *yomichigaeru*<br>to misread | 読み違える |

Following are examples in sentence form.

(1) スーパーへ行ったのに、野菜を買い忘れた。[買う *kau*]
*Sūpā e itta no ni, yasai o kaiwasureta.*
I went to the supermarket, but I forgot to buy vegetables.

きのう提出した書類に、判を押し忘れた。[押す *osu*]
*Kinō teishutsu shita shorui ni, han o oshiwasureta.*
I forgot to put my seal on the documents I submitted yesterday.

(2) 多田さんの住所を書き落した。[書く *kaku*]
*Tada-san no jūsho o kakiotoshita.*
I left off Mrs. Tada's address. (I failed to write down Mrs. Tada's address.)

In the next example, the noun お見落とし *o-miotoshi* is derived from the verb 見落とす *miotosu*.

年次報告書の2頁、お見落としのないようによくごらんください。[見る *miru*]
*Nenji hōkoku-sho no ni-pēji, o-miotoshi no nai yō ni yoku goran kudasai.*
Please take a good look at page two of the annual report without fail.

(3) 漢字を読み間違えてしまった。[読む *yomu*]
*Kanji o yomimachigaete shimatta.*
I misread the kanji.

その子供があんまり大きくなって、見違えてしまった。
*Sono kodomo ga ammari ōkiku natte, michigaete shimatta.*
The child has gotten so big I almost didn't recognize her.

## Entering and Inserting 中に入る、中に入れる ━━━

| | |
|---|---|
| /-~~masu~~/ + komu | /－~~ます~~/ ＋込む |
| nage/~~masu~~/komu | 投げ/~~ます~~/込む |

This ending expresses the idea of entering something or putting one thing inside another.

選手は合図に合わせて、プールに飛び込んだ。[飛ぶ *tobu*]

*Senshu wa aizu ni awasete, pūru ni tobikonda.*

At the signal, the swimmers dove into the pool.

ご住所とお名前を、この書類にボールペンで書き込んでいただきたいんですが。[書く *kaku*]

*Gojūsho to o-namae o, kono shorui ni bōrupen de kaki-konde itadakitai n' desu ga.*

I would like you to fill in your name and address on this form with a ballpoint pen.

## Getting Used to an Action 何かに慣れる ━━━

| | |
|---|---|
| /-~~masu~~/ + nareru | /－~~ます~~/ ＋慣れる |
| mi/~~masu~~/nareru | 見/~~ます~~/慣れる |

The ending *nareru* 慣れる expresses the idea of becoming accustomed to an action.

やっとこの靴、はき慣れて歩きやすくなった。[はく *haku*]

*Yatto kono kutsu, hakinarete arukiyasuku natta.*

I've finally gotten used to wearing these shoes, so now they're easy to walk in.

毎日見慣れた通りなのに、朝早くだと違って見える。 [見る *miru*]

*Mainichi minareta tōri na no ni, asa hayaku da to chi-gatte mieru.*

I'm used to seeing this street every day, but early in the morning it looks different.

## Redoing or Rechecking an Action
もう一度する、調べる ━━━━━━━━━━

| | |
|---|---|
| /-~~masu~~/ + naosu | /ー~~ます~~/ + 直す |
| yomi/~~masu~~/naosu | 読み/~~ます~~/直す |

This ending means to redo or recheck something.

作文を書いたら、読み直して下さい。 [読む *yomu*]

*Sakubun o kaitara, yominaoshite kudasai.*

After you write your composition, please read it over again.

青木はただいま会議中ですので、後でお電話かけ直していただけませんか。 [かける *kakeru*]

*Aoki wa tadaima kaigi-chū desu no de, ato de o-denwa kakenaoshite itadakemasen ka.*

Mr. Aoki is now in a meeting. Could you please call back again later?

## Mutual Action 互いに何かをする ━━━━━━━━

| | |
|---|---|
| /-~~masu~~/ + au | /ー~~ます~~/ + 合う |
| oshie/~~masu~~/au | 教え/~~ます~~/合う |

This ending means to do something mutually or reciprocally.

その二人は心から愛し合っていた。 [愛する *aisuru*]

*Sono futari wa kokoro kara aishiatte ita.*

Those two sincerely loved each other.

山本さんの兄弟は早く両親に死なれたので、助け合って暮らしている。 [助ける *tasukeru*]

*Yamamoto-san no kyōdai wa hayaku ryōshin ni shinareta no de, tasukeatte kurashite iru.*

The Yamamoto brothers lost their parents early on, so now they live by helping each other.

## Excessive Action 過剰 ━━━━━━

| | |
|---|---|
| /-~~masu~~/ + suguru | /ー~~ます~~/ + 過ぎる |
| nomi/~~masu~~/suguru | 飲み/~~ます~~/過ぎる |

This ending indicates that something is done to excess.

安倍さんはタバコを吸いすぎますね。 [吸う *suu*]
*Abe-san wa tabako o suisugimasu ne.*
Mr. Abe smokes too much, doesn't he.

昨晩の宴会で飲み過ぎて、今朝は二日酔いだ。[飲む
*nomu*]
*Sakuban no enkai de nomisugite, kesa wa futsukayoi da.*
I drank too much at the banquet yesterday, so this morning I have a hangover.

## Attaching Actions 接触する、くっつく ━━━━━

| | |
|---|---|
| (1) /-~~masu~~/ + tsuku | /ー~~ます~~/ + つく |
| tobi/~~masu~~/tsuku | 飛び/~~ます~~/つく [to fly onto, to jump onto] |
| (2) /-~~masu~~/ + tsukeru | /ー~~ます~~/ + つける |
| yobi/~~masu~~/tsukeru | 呼び/~~ます~~/つける [to summon (someone to oneself)] |

These endings describe the actions of approaching or attaching onto something.

(1) 犬はその女の子に飛びついた。 [飛ぶ *tobu*]
*Inu wa sono onna no ko ni tobitsuita.*
The dog jumped up onto the girl.

急いで歩いて行ったら、谷さんにすぐ追いつきましたよ。
[追う *ou*]
*Isoide aruite ittara, Tani-san ni sugu oitsukimashita yo.*
By walking quickly, I soon caught up with Ms. Tani.

(2)幼稚園の子供の上着には、名前が縫いつけてあります。
[縫う *nuu*]

*Yōchi-en no kodomo no uwagi ni wa, namae ga nui-tsukete arimasu.*

The children's names are sewn onto their nursery school jackets.

きのうは書類の書き方を間違えたので、課長に呼びつけられてどなられた。[呼ぶ *yobu*]

*Kinō wa shorui no kakikata o machigaeta no de, kachō ni yobitsukerarete donarareta.*

Yesterday I made a mistake in writing some documents, so I was called onto the carpet by the section chief.

## Going or Coming for a Purpose 動作の目的 ─────

| | |
|---|---|
| (1) /-~~masu~~/ + *ni iku* | ／ー~~ます~~／＋に行く |
| *tabe/~~masu~~/ ni iku* | 食べ／~~ます~~／に行く |
| (2) /-~~masu~~/ + *ni kuru* | ／ー~~ます~~／＋に来る |
| *nomi/~~masu~~/ ni kuru* | 飲み／~~ます~~／に来る |

The endings *ni iku* に行く and *ni kuru* に来る express the idea of going or coming in order to do something.

(1)明日は映画を見に行くつもりです。[見る *miru*]

*Ashita wa eiga o mi ni iku tsumori desu.*

I plan to go see a movie tomorrow.

社長は一時に運輸大臣に会いに行って、三時には成田へ会長を送りに行く予定だ。[会う *au*, 送る *okuru*]

*Shachō wa ichiji ni Un'yu Daijin ni ai ni itte, sanji ni wa Narita e kaichō o okuri ni iku yotei da.*

The company president is scheduled to go meet the Minister of Transport at one o'clock and then go to Narita to see off the chairman of the board at three.

(2)このレストランは安くておいしいから、毎日大勢のお客が食べに来る。

*Kono resutoran wa yasukute oishii kara, mainichi ōzei no o-kyaku ga tabe ni kuru.*

This restaurant has cheap, tasty food, so many customers come to eat here every day.

最近は中国など、アジアから勉強をしに来る留学生が多くなった。[する *suru*]
*Saikin wa Chūgoku nado, Ajia kara benkyō o shi ni kuru ryūgakusei ga ōku natta.*

Lately, many more foreign students from China and other parts of Asia have been coming here to study.

## Going, Coming, or Returning After Doing Something 動作の連続

| | |
|---|---|
| (1) *-te + iku* | ー て ＋ 行く |
| *kaite iku* | 書いて行く |
| to write and go | |
| (2) *-te + kuru* | ー て ＋ 来る |
| *wasurete kuru* | 忘れて来る |
| to forget and come | |
| (3) *-te + kaeru* | ー て ＋ 帰る |
| *katte kaeru* | 買って帰る |
| to buy and go back | |

When used after the *-te* form, the endings *iku* 行く, *kuru* 来る, and *kaeru* 帰る indicate that the subject has gone, come, or returned home, to the office, etc. after the action of the first verb was completed.

(1) これを持って行って下さい。[持つ *motsu*]
*Kore o motte itte kudasai.*
Please take this with you.

ここに伝言を書いて行けば、遅く来た人はこれを読むでしょう。[書く *kaku*]
*Koko ni dengon o kaite ikeba, osoku kita hito wa kore o yomu deshō.*
If we write a message here before we leave, the people who come late will read it.

(2) 宿題を持って来ましたか。 [持つ *motsu*]

*Shukudai o motte kimashita ka.*

Did you bring your homework?

来る途中でビールを買って来るように山本さんに頼んだよ。 [買う *kau*]

*Kuru tochū de bīru o katte kuru yō ni Yamamoto-san ni tanonda yo.*

I asked Miss Yamamoto to buy some beer on her way here.

(3) おみやげを買って帰った。 [買う *kau*]

*Omiyage o katte kaetta.*

I brought back some souvenirs I'd bought.

このところ、課長は毎晩のように飲んで帰るらしいよ。 [飲む *nomu*]

*Kono tokoro, kachō wa maiban no yō ni nonde kaeru rashii yo.*

Lately, it seems that our section chief goes out drinking every night before going home.

## Gradual Change ゆっくり変化する状態 ━━━━━

| | |
|---|---|
| (1) /-*te*/ + *iku* | ／ーて／＋いく |
| *natte iku* | なっていく |
| to become gradually | |
| (2) /-*te*/ + *kuru* | ／ーて／＋くる |
| *dekite kuru* | できてくる |
| to become able gradually | |

These endings indicate a gradual change. In this case the verbs *iku* いく and *kuru* くる do not literally mean "to go" or "to come," so they are normally written in hiragana instead of as 行く or 来る. While they can be used interchangeably, the former implies an objective judgment, the latter a subjective viewpoint.

(1) だんだん熱が下がっていくでしょう。 [下がる *sagaru*]
*Dandan netsu ga sagatte iku deshō.*
Your fever should gradually go down.

春になれば雪も溶けていくだろう。 [溶ける *tokeru*]
*Haru ni nareba yuki mo tokete iku darō.*
When spring comes, the snow will slowly melt away.

(2) あたりがだんだん暗くなってきた。 [なる *naru*]
*Atari ga dandan kuraku natte kita.*
It's been getting darker around here.

建築中のマンション、だいぶできてきましたね。 [できる *dekiru*]
*Kenchiku-chū no manshon, daibu dekite kimashita ne.*
That condo under construction has really begun to take shape.

# 4

# Useful Expressions

Japanese is full of fixed expressions that convey a wide range of useful meanings. Because many of these expressions consist of specific combinations of inflected verb forms, particles, and other words, they are often difficult to look up in dictionaries. This chapter presents some of the most common of these expressions.

## -Ba ...hodo ーば ...ほど

| | |
|---|---|
| *-ba* + plain form + *hodo* | ーば ＋ 原形 ＋ ほど |
| *mireba miru hodo* | 見れば見るほど |

This pattern describes properties that grow stronger as the action of the verb progresses. The same verb appears twice, first in the *-ba* form and then in the plain form followed by *hodo* ほど.

森下：あの白い花、きれいですね。
奈良：本当に、見れば見るほどきれいな花ですね。
*Morishita: Ano shiroi hana, kirei desu ne.*
*Nara: Hontō ni, mireba miru hodo kirei na hana desu ne.*
Morishita: Those white flowers are really pretty.
Nara: That's so true. The more you look at them, the prettier they seem.

ブレナン：日本では地方によって気温がちがいますね。
中田：ふつう北へ行けば行くほど涼しくなりますよ。

*Brennan: Nihon de wa chihō ni yotte kion ga chigaimasu ne.*

*Nakata: Futsū kita e ikeba iku hodo suzushiku narimasu yo.*

Brennan: In Japan, the temperature is quite different depending on the part of the country.

Nakata: Generally, the farther north you go, the cooler it gets.

## Dake atte だけあって ━━━━━━━━━━━━

| | |
|---|---|
| plain form/-*ta* + *dake atte* | 原形／ーた＋だけあって |
| *kuru (kita) dake atte* | 来る（来た）だけあって |

This pattern is used to show that one action or property follows naturally from another. The phrase *dake atte* だけあって is preceded by the plain form or the informal past tense.

南：小田先生はノーベル賞をもらっただけあって、さすがに頭のいい方ですね。[もらう *morau*]

小笠原：それにお人柄もすばらしいかたです。

*Minami: Oda-sensei wa Nōberu Shō o moratta dake atte, sasuga ni atama no ii kata desu ne.*

*Ogasawara: Sore ni o-hitogara mo subarashii kata desu.*

Minami: Professor Oda has a fine mind, just what you'd expect of a Nobel Prize winner.

Ogasawara: She is also a person of exceptional character.

北海道の一番北へ来ただけあって、寒さは厳しいですね。[来る *kuru*]

*Hokkaidō no ichiban kita e kita dake atte, samusa wa kibishii desu ne.*

Just as you'd expect after coming to the northernmost tip of Hokkaido, it is extremely cold.

## Dake demo だけでも, dake (wa) だけ(は) ━━━━━

| | |
|---|---|
| plain form + *dake demo /dake wa / dake* | 原形＋だけでも／だけは／だけ |
| *taberu dake demo* | 食べるだけでも |

| | |
|---|---|
| *taberu dake wa* | 食べるだけは |
| *taberu dake* | 食べるだけ |

This pattern expresses the notion of doing as much as one can under the circumstances. The plain form precedes *dake demo* だけでも, *dake wa* だけは, or just *dake* だけ.

小池：その店は本当に安いんですか。
板橋：安いと言う評判なんですが、まあ行くだけでも行ってみましょう。

*Koike: Sono mise wa hontō ni yasui n' desu ka.*
*Itabashi: Yasui to yū hyōban nan desu ga, mā iku dake demo itte mimashō.*

Koike: Is that restaurant really cheap?
Itabashi: It has that reputation, but why don't we just try going to see what it's like?

坂田：谷さんはいつも勤務時間に遅れて来ますね。
関口：注意するだけはしたんですが、全然きかないんですよ。

*Sakata: Tani-san wa itsumo kimmu jikan ni okurete ki-masu ne.*
*Sekiguchi: Chūi suru dake wa shita n' desu ga, zenzen kikanai n' desu yo.*

Sakata: Mr. Tani is always late for work.
Sekiguchi: I did my best to warn him about it, but it didn't do any good.

## -Gachi ーがち

| | |
|---|---|
| */-masu/ + gachi* | ／ーます／＋がち |
| *wasure/masu/gachi* | 忘れ／ます／がち |

This suffix, attached to the */-masu/* stem, indicates a tendency or habitual characteristic.

寺田：いつお会いしてもお若いですね。
林：とんでもない。この頃は何でも忘れがちになって、困っています。[忘れる *wasureru*]

*Terada: Itsu o-ai shite mo o-wakai desu ne.*

*Hayashi: Tondemonai. Kono goro wa nan de mo wasure-gachi ni natte, komatte imasu.*

Terada: No matter when I see you, you seem as young as ever.

Hayashi: Not at all. Lately I've become so forgetful that it's embarrassing.

東京地方は曇りがちの天気です。 [曇る *kumoru*]
*Tōkyō chihō wa kumorigachi no tenki desu.*
The weather in the Tokyo area will be mostly cloudy.

## Gurai nara ...hō ga ii ぐらいなら〜方がいい ━━━━

> plain form + *gurai nara* + plain form/*-ta* + *hō ga ii* / *hō ga mashi da*
>
> 原形 + ぐらいなら + 原形／ーた + ほうがいい／ほうがましだ
>
> *morau gurai nara shinu (shinda) hō ga ii/mashi da*
> もらうぐらいなら死ぬ（死んだ）ほうがいい／ほうがましだ

This pattern expresses the notion that "it's better to do this than that," the former seen as the lesser of two evils. The phrase is also used rhetorically, as in the first example below. The verb before *gurai nara* ぐらいなら is the plain form, while the verb before *hō ga ii* 方がいい can be either the plain form or informal past (*-ta*).

As shown in the following examples, *gurai nara* ぐらいなら has the alternate form *kurai nara* くらいなら, and *hō ga ii* 方がいい can be replaced by *hō ga mashi da* 方がましだ, which, however, is more colloquial and blunter.

兄にお金をもらうくらいなら、死んだ方がいい。 [死ぬ *shinu*]
*Ani ni o-kane o morau kurai nara, shinda hō ga ii.*
I'd rather die than take money from my older brother.

戦争に行って死ぬぐらいなら、逃げる方がましです。
*Sensō ni itte shinu gurai nara, nigeru hō ga mashi desu.*

It's better to make a run for it than go off and die in war.

## Ikura -te mo ... -nai いくら ーても 〜ーない ━━━━

| | |
|---|---|
| *ikura + -te mo + -nai* | いくら＋ーても＋ーない |
| *ikura mite mo akinai* | いくら見ても飽きない |

The first half of this pattern *ikura -te mo* いくら ーても corresponds to the English "no matter how much I did (or do) something." The verb in the next clause must be negative.

岸：本、見つかりました？
上野：それがいくら探しても見つからないんですよ。[探
　　　す *sagasu*, 見つかる *mitsukaru*]
*Kishi: Hon, mitsukarimashita?*
*Ueno: Sore ga ikura sagashite mo mitsukaranai n' desu yo.*
Kishi: Did you find the book?
Ueno: No matter how much I look for it, I can't find it.

いくら歩いても山小屋に着かなかった。[歩く *aruku*, 着く
　　*tsuku*]
*Ikura aruite mo yamagoya ni tsukanakatta.*
No matter how much we walked, we didn't reach the
　　mountain cabin.

## To ieba と言えば ━━━━━━━━━

| | |
|---|---|
| plain form/noun + *to ieba* | 原形／名詞＋と言えば |
| *utau (uta) to ieba* | 歌う（歌）といえば |

This pattern is used to introduce a new topic related to something that has already been mentioned. Either a plain form verb or a noun may precede *to ieba* と言えば.

池田：雨が降らないと言えば、もう一ヶ月も降りません
　　　ね。[降る *furu*]
田村：そうですね。水不足にならなければいいですが。
*Ikeda: Ame ga furanai to ieba, mō ikkagetsu mo furi-*
　　*masen ne.*

*Tamura: Sō desu ne. Mizubusoku ni naranakereba ii desu ga.*

Ikeda: Speaking of the lack of rain, it hasn't rained for a full month now, has it.

Tamura: That's right. I hope we don't have a water shortage.

大山：きのう高田さんに会いましたよ。よろしく言ってました。

岩崎：ありがとう。高田と言えばまだゴルフやってるかなあ。

*Ōyama: Kinō Takada-san ni aimashita yo. Yoroshiku itte 'mashita.*

*Iwasaki: Arigatō. Takada to ieba mada gorufu yatte 'ru ka nā.*

Ōyama: I saw Mr. Takada yesterday. He said to say hello.

Iwasaki: Thanks. Now that you mention him, I wonder if he still plays golf.

## To itte mo ii hodo da　と言ってもいいほどだ ━━━

| plain form /-ta/noun + | 原形／ーた／名詞 + |
|---|---|
| *to itte mo ii hodo da* | と言ってもいいほどだ |
| *ensō o shita to itte mo ii hodo da* | 演奏をしたといってもいいほどだ |
| *saidai no higai to itte mo ii hodo da* | 最大の被害といってもいいほどだ |

This pattern is similar to the English "you could even go so far as to say that...." The phrase above is preceded by a plain form verb or a noun.

Note that *itte* 言って is also pronounced *yutte* in conversation.

町田：あのピアニストの演奏、すばらしかったですね。

望月：今年一番すばらしい演奏をしたと言ってもいいほどですよ。[する *suru*]

*Machida: Ano pianisto no ensō, subarashikatta desu ne.*

*Mochizuki: Kotoshi ichiban subarashii ensō o shita to itte mo ii hodo desu yo.*

Machida: The pianist's performance was wonderful, wasn't it?

Mochizuki: You could even say that he gave the best performance of the year.

松崎：この前の地震、ひどかったですね。

中島：戦後最大の被害だと言ってもいいほどでしょう。

*Matsuzaki: Kono mae no jishin, hidokatta desu ne.*

*Nakajima: Sengo saidai no higai da to yutte mo ii hodo deshō.*

Matsuzaki: The recent earthquake was really terrible.

Nakajima: Without exaggeration, you could probably say it was the worst since the end of war.

## Wa iu made mo naku は言うまでもなく ━━━━

| | |
|---|---|
| noun + *wa iu made mo naku* | 名詞 + は言うまでもなく |
| *kodomo wa iu made mo naku* | 子供は言うまでもなく |

This pattern corresponds to the first half of the English expression "not only … but also." The Japanese phrase corresponding to "but also" uses *mo* も in place of *wa* は.

梅津：内田さんご兄弟は、お兄さんは言うまでもなく、
弟さんも優秀ですね。

永田：そうなんですよ。あのご兄弟は子供の時から頭が
良くて評判でした。

*Umezu: Uchida-san go-kyōdai wa, onīsan wa iu made mo naku, otōto-san mo yūshū desu ne.*

*Nagata: Sō nan desu yo. Ano go-kyōdai wa kodomo no toki kara atama ga yokute hyōban deshita.*

Umezu: The Uchida brothers are really exceptional—not only the older brother, of course, but the younger one, too.

Nagata: That's very true. Both of them have had the reputation of being bright ever since they were children.

このスポーツは若い人は言うまでもなく、お年寄りにも
楽しんでいただけます。

*Kono supōtsu wa wakai hito wa iu made mo naku, o-toshiyori ni mo tanoshinde itadakemasu.*

This sport can be enjoyed not only by the young but by the elderly as well.

## To iu yori wa mushiro と言うよりはむしろ ────

| | |
|---|---|
| noun + *to iu yori wa mushiro* | 名詞 + と言うよりはむしろ |
| *gakusei to iu yori wa mushiro* | 学生と言うよりはむしろ |

This pattern is used to say "not so much this as that." Usually a noun precedes the *to* と.

森さんは学者と言うよりはむしろ政治家です。
*Mori-san wa gakusha to iu yori wa mushiro seijika desu.*
Mr. Mori is not so much a scholar as a politician.

この作品は小説と言うよりはむしろ詩といった方がいいでしょう。
*Kono sakuhin wa shōsetsu to iu yori wa mushiro shi to itta hō ga ii deshō.*
It would be better to call this work a poem than a novel.

## (To iu) wake de wa nai (と言う)わけではない ────

| | |
|---|---|
| plain form + *(to iu) wake de wa nai* | 原形 + (と言う)わけではない |
| *ikanai (to iu) wake de wa nai* | 行かない（と言う）わけではない |

This pattern, used after the plain form, corresponds roughly to "it's not that...."

前田：来月の社員旅行いらっしゃらないんですか。
高橋：行かないと言うわけではないんだが、あまり気が進まなくてね。 [行く *iku*]
*Maeda: Raigetsu no shain ryokō irassharanai n' desu ka.*

*Takahashi: Ikanai to iu wake de wa nai n' da ga, amari ki
ga susumanakute ne.*

Maeda: Won't you be going on the employee trip next
month?

Takahashi: I don't mean to say that I won't be going, but
I'm not feeling very enthusiastic about it.

自民党はその案に反対しているわけではない。

*Jimin-tō wa sono an ni hantai shite iru wake de wa nai.*

The Liberal Democratic Party is not necessarily opposed
to the proposal.

## A kara B ni kakete　AからBにかけて ━━━━━━

| noun + *kara* + noun + *ni kakete* | 名詞 + から + 名詞 + にかけて |
|---|---|
| *ashita kara asatte ni kakete* | あしたからあさってにかけて |

This pattern means "from A and into B," where A and B
are nouns of time or place.

あしたからあさってにかけて、台風が近づきますので、
関東地方は強い風と雨に見舞われる恐れがあります。

*Ashita kara asatte ni kakete, taifū ga chikazukimasu no
de, Kantō chihō wa tsuyoi kaze to ame ni mimawareru
osore ga arimasu.*

A typhoon is approaching, so there is a danger that the
Kantō region will be hit by strong winds and rain tomorrow and into the next day.

今週末から来週にかけて、大蔵大臣は中国を訪問する予
定だ。

*Konshūmatsu kara raishū ni kakete, Ōkura Daijin wa
Chūgoku o hōmon suru yotei da.*

The Minister of Finance is scheduled to visit China this
weekend and early next week.

## To kuraberu to と比べると ━━━━━━

> noun + *to/ni kuraberu to* 名詞 + と／に比べると
> *mukashi to/ni kuraberu to* 昔と／に比べると

This pattern means "compared to...." The particle may be either *to* と or *ni* に.

片山：昔と比べると、この辺もずいぶんにぎやかになりましたね。

村上：そうですね、10年前はこの辺は畑ばかりでしたものね。

*Katayama: Mukashi to kuraberu to, kono hen mo zuibun nigiyaka ni narimashita ne.*

*Murakami: Sō desu ne, jūnen mae wa kono hen wa hatake bakari deshita mono ne.*

Katayama: Compared to the old days, this area has really livened up, hasn't it?

Murakami: It sure has. Ten years ago, there was nothing but farms around here.

街中に比べると、この辺は静かですね。

*Machinaka ni kuraberu to, kono hen wa shizuka desu ne.*

Compared to the city, this area certainly is quiet.

## O kagiri ni を限りに ━━━━━━

> noun + *o kagiri ni* 名詞 + を限りに
> *kotoshi o kagiri ni* 今年を限りに

This pattern specifies the time when something ends or changes fundamentally.

岡部：河村さん今学期を限りに大学をやめるそうですね。

間島：でも来年は留学するそうですよ。

*Okabe: Kawamura-san kongakki o kagiri ni daigaku o yameru sō desu ne.*

*Majima: Demo rainen wa ryūgaku suru sō desu yo.*

Okabe: I hear that Ms. Kawamura is going to drop out of school at the end of this semester.

Majima: But then I heard that she's going abroad to study next year.

二人はその日を限りに、二度と会わなかった。
*Futari wa sono hi o kagiri ni, nido to awanakatta.*
The two never met again after that day.

## Kagiri wa かぎりは

| | |
|---|---|
| plain form + *kagiri wa* | 原形 + かぎりは |
| *akiramenai kagiri wa* | 諦めない限りは [諦める to give up] |

This phrase corresponds to the English "as long as." It follows the plain form (often negative) of the verb.

浅野：おたくの犬、怖そうですが、かみつくことはありませんか。
安藤：こちらがいじめたりしない限りは、大丈夫ですよ。[する *suru*]

*Asano: Otaku no inu, kowasō desu ga, kamitsuku koto wa arimasen ka.*
*Andō: Kochira ga ijimetari shinai kagiri wa, daijōbu desu yo.*

Asano: Your dog looks mean. Does he ever bite?
Andō: He's okay as long as you don't treat him bad.

台風でも来ないかぎり、試合は中止しません。[来る *kuru*]
*Taifū de mo konai kagiri wa, shiai wa chūshi shimasen.*
The game won't be cancelled as long as a typhoon or something like that doesn't come along.

## Ka to omou to / ka to omottara かと思うと／かと思ったら

| | |
|---|---|
| *-ta + ka to omou to* | ーた + かと思うと |
| *ame ga futta ka to omou to* | 雨が降ったかと思うと |
| *-ta + ka to omottara* | ーた + かと思ったら |
| *ame ga futta ka to omottara* | 雨が降ったかと思ったら |

These patterns mean "as soon as." In either case, the phrase follows the informal past tense.

空が暗くなったかと思うと、大粒の雨が降り出した。[なる *naru*]

*Sora ga kuraku natta ka to omou to, ōtsubu no ame ga furidashita.*

No sooner had the sky turned dark than large raindrops began to fall.

ベッドに入ったかと思ったら、もう眠ってしまった。 [入る *hairu*]

*Beddo ni haitta ka to omottara, mō nemutte shimatta.*

He fell asleep as soon as he got into bed.

## Kanarazu shi mo … to wa kagiranai / to wa ienai
### 必ずしも〜とは限らない／とは言えない

| | |
|---|---|
| *kanarazu shi mo* + plain form + *to wa kagiranai* | 必ずしも＋原形＋とは限らない |
| *kanarazu shi mo iku to wa kagiranai* | 必ずしも行くとは限らない |
| *kanarazu shi mo* + plain form + *to wa ienai* | 必ずしも＋原形＋とは言えない |
| *kanarazu shi mo sō to wa ienai* | 必ずしもそうとは言えない |

This pattern means "it isn't necessarily so." The *to wa kagiranai* とは限らない is preceded by a plain form verb or, when the topic has already been mentioned, the demonstrative pronoun *sō* そう.

内藤：この頃の若い人はみんな大学へ行くんでしょう。

和田：必ずしも行くとは限らないでしょう。勉強が嫌いな若者もいますから。

*Naitō: Konogoro no wakai hito wa minna daigaku e iku n' deshō.*

*Wada: Kanarazu shi mo iku to wa kagiranai deshō. Benkyō ga kirai na wakamono mo imasu kara.*

Naitō: These days, I suppose all young people go to college.

Wada: They don't necessarily all go. After all, some young people don't like studying.

深山：両親が頭がいいと、子供も頭がいいんでしょうね。

吉田：必ずしもそうとは言えないようですよ。

*Fukayama: Ryōshin ga atama ga ii to, kodomo mo atama ga ii n' deshō ne.*

*Yoshida: Kanarazu shi mo sō to wa ienai yō desu yo.*

Fukayama: If the parents are bright, then the children will be bright, too, won't they.

Yoshida: That doesn't seem to apply in every case.

## Kaneru ーかねる

| | |
|---|---|
| /-~~masu~~/ + *kaneru* | ー／~~ます~~／＋かねる |
| *deki*/~~masu~~/*kaneru* | でき／~~ます~~／かねる |

This suffix often translates as "cannot," but with the nuance of "unable to endure" or "unable to accept," and it often indicates that something cannot be done or is difficult to do even with the best of wills. It attaches to the */-masu/* stem.

広瀬：この間お願いしました件は、いかがでしょうか。お引き受け願えますでしょうか。

藤原：それが、社長とも相談いたしましたが、私どもではお引き受けできかねると申しておりました。どうぞご了承下さい。[できる *dekiru*]

*Hirose: Kono aida onegai shimashita ken wa, ikaga deshō ka. O-hikiuke negaemasu deshō ka.*

*Fujiwara: Sore ga, shachō to mo sōdan itashimashita ga, watakushi-domo de wa o-hikiuke dekikaneru to mōshite orimashita. Dōzo go-ryōshō kudasai.*

Hirose: How about that matter we proposed recently? Will you be able to undertake it?

Fujiwara: The fact is, I consulted with our president about it, but he said that we would be unable to comply. Please understand our situation.

本間：あの国には物売りの子供がたくさんいたでしょう。

菊池：いたわよ。街の中でね、小学校にも行っていない
　　　ような小さな子供が花を売っていたの。かわいそうで
　　　しょう。見かねてついお金を上げてしまったのよ。[見
　　　る *miru*]

*Homma: Ano kuni ni wa monouri no kodomo ga takusan ita deshō.*

*Kikuchi: Ita wa yo. Machi no naka de ne, shōgakkō ni mo itte inai yō na chiisana kodomo ga hana o utte ita no. Kawaisō deshō. Mikanete tsui o-kane o agete shimatta no yo.*

Homma: There must have been a lot of children trying to sell things in that country.

Kikuchi (female): Yes, there were. Kids who looked too small even for elementary school were selling flowers on the street. It's such a shame, don't you think. I couldn't bear to look anymore, so I gave them some money.

## Ni kakawarazu にかかわらず ━━━━━━━━━

| affirmative plain form + negative plain form + *ni kakawarazu* | 肯定原形＋否定原形＋に かかわらず |
|---|---|
| *iku ikanai ni kakawarazu* | 行く行かないにかかわ らず |

This pattern means "regardless of whether or not...." The phrase *ni kakawarazu* にかかわらず is preceded by the same verb twice, first in the plain affirmative form and then in the plain negative.

旅行に行く行かないにかかわらず、皆さん説明だけはお
聞きになってください。

*Ryokō ni iku ikanai ni kakawarazu, mina-san setsumei dake wa o-kiki ni natte kudasai.*

Please listen to my explanation whether or not you will be going on the trip.

食事をするしないにかかわらず、会費は一万円です。

*Shokuji o suru shinai ni kakawarazu, kaihi wa ichiman en desu.*

The fee is 10,000 yen regardless of whether you eat or not.

## Koto wa nai　ことはない

| | |
|---|---|
| *-ta + koto wa nai* | ―た＋ことはない |
| *itta koto wa nai* | 行ったことはない |

This pattern is used to emphasize that one has never done something. It is the negative version of the pattern mentioned on page 68 for describing one's experience.

土屋：遅いわね、林さん。もしかしたら来ないんじゃない。
関：来るわよ。あの人これまで約束破ったことはないから。[破る *yaburu*]

*Tsuchiya: Osoi wa ne, Hayashi-san. Moshikashitara konai n' ja nai.*

*Seki: Kuru wa yo. Ano hito kore made yakusoku yabutta koto wa nai kara.*

Tsuchiya: Ms. Hayashi is really late. Maybe she's not going to come.

Seki (female): She'll come. She has never once broken a promise.

政治家は一般に選挙前に約束したことを実行したことはない。[する *suru*]

*Seiji-ka wa ippan ni senkyo mae ni yakusoku shita koto o jikkō shita koto wa nai.*

Politicians generally never keep the promises that they make before elections.

## Koto ni wa　ことには

| | |
|---|---|
| *-nai + koto ni wa* | ―ない＋ことには |
| *ikanai koto ni wa* | 行かないことには [until (unless) you go] |
| *-ta + koto ni wa* | ―た＋ことには |
| *akireta koto ni wa* | あきれたことには [to my astonishment] |

This pattern (*koto ni wa*) is a nominalizer, that is, it allows a verb to be treated as a noun in the sentence. It follows the plain present negative or informal past form of the verb, affirmative or negative. With a negative verb, it contains the meaning that "unless something has been done, or is done, something else will not follow." With an affirmative verb, it emphasizes a verb expressing emotion.

新村：あの子の描く絵、本当にすばらしいのよ。
西田：そうなの、見ないことには何とも言えないけど。
[見る *miru*]

*Niimura: Ano ko no kaku e, hontō ni subarashii no yo.*
*Nishida: Sō na no, minai koto ni wa nan to mo ienai kedo.*

Niimura: The pictures drawn by that child are truly amazing.
Nishida: Is that so? Without seeing them, I really couldn't say.

驚いたことには、松本さんがきのう亡くなったそうです。
[驚く *odoroku*]

*Odoroita koto ni wa, Matsumoto-san ga kinō nakunatta sō desu.*

I was surprised to hear that Mr. Matsumoto passed away yesterday.

## Koto mo nai こともない

| | |
|---|---|
| -nai + koto mo nai | ーない＋こともない |
| kawanai koto mo nai | 買わないこともない |

This negative pattern is used after the plain negative form of the verb. The resulting double negative is a weak affirmative that leaves some doubt about whether the action of the verb will actually take place.

青木：この前見に行ったマンション、お買いになるんですか。
杉本：値段によっては買わないこともないんですが……
[買う *kau*]

*Aoki: Kono mae mi ni itta manshon, o-kai ni naru n' desu ka.*

*Sugimoto: Nedan ni yotte wa kawanai koto mo nai n'
desu ga...*

Aoki: Are you going to buy that condominium you went
to look at the other day?

Sugimoto: Well, we may end up buying it, depending on
the price.

丸田：佐藤さんと鈴木さん、結婚しそうですか。

笹山：佐藤さんの気持ちしだいで、結婚しないこともな
いような気がしますけど。

*Maruta: Satō-san to Suzuki-san, kekkon shisō desu ka.*

*Sasayama: Satō-san no kimochi shidai de, kekkon shinai
koto mo nai yō na ki ga shimasu kedo.*

Maruta: Does it seem likely that Miss Satō and Mr.
Suzuki will get married?

Sasayama: It all depends on how Miss Satō feels. It
wouldn't surprise me if they did get married.

## Koto wa ... ga ことは〜が

| | |
|---|---|
| *-ta + koto wa + -ta + ga* | ーた＋ことは＋ーた＋が |
| *itta koto wa itta ga* | 行ったことは行ったが |

In this pattern, the same verb appears twice in the informal past form, once before *koto wa* ことは and once before
*ga* が. It expresses the idea that, despite one's best effort, the
result was bad.

桑原：きのうの映画良かったですか。

田村：それが、行ったことは行ったんですが、混んでい
て入れなかったんですよ。

*Kuwahara: Kinō no eiga yokatta desu ka.*

*Tamura: Sore ga, itta koto wa itta n' desu ga, konde ite
hairenakatta n' desu yo.*

Kuwahara: Was the movie any good yesterday?

Tamura: As a matter of fact, I did go to see it, but it was
so crowded that I couldn't get in.

中田さん、手術を受けたことは受けたらしいんですが、だ
めだったそうです。[受ける *ukeru*]

*Nakata-san, shujutsu o uketa koto wa uketa rashii n' desu ga, dame datta sō desu.*

It seems that Mr. Nakata did have an operation, but apparently it turned out badly.

## -Nai uchi wa ーないうちは

| | |
|---|---|
| *-nai uchi wa* | ーない＋うちは |
| *shinai uchi wa* | しないうちは |

Translated literally, this pattern means "while the action does not occur," but a better rendition into English is "until."

この仕事を片づけないうちは出かけられない。 [片づける *katatsukeru*]
*Kono shigoto o katazukenai uchi wa dekakerarenai.*
We can't leave until we finish up this work.

This pattern appears in the following well-known proverb:

日光を見ないうちは結構とはいえない。 [見る *miru*]
*Nikkō o minai uchi wa kekkō to wa ienai.*
You can't say "Splendid!" until you've seen Nikkō.

The proverb refers to 東照宮 *Tōshōgū*, which is located in Nikkō in Tochigi Prefecture. This splendidly decorated seventeenth-century shrine is the burial place of 徳川家康 *Tokugawa Ieyasu*, the first shogun. The proverb also plays on the rhyme between *Nikkō* and *kekkō*.

## Ni wa oyobanai には及ばない

| | |
|---|---|
| plain form + *ni wa oyobanai* | 原形＋には及ばない |
| *deru in wa oyobanai* | 出るには及ばない |

This pattern indicates that something is unnecessary, superfluous, or of insufficient importance to call for a certain action. It follows the plain form of the verb.

加藤：明日は組合の全体会議があるそうですね。みんな出なくっちゃならないんですかね。

金原：忙しいんだから、みんな出るには及ばないだろう。

*Katō: Ashita wa kumiai no zentai kaigi ga aru sō desu ne.*
*Minna denakutcha naranai n' desu ka ne.*

*Kanehara: Isogashii n' da kara, minna deru ni wa oyo-*
*banai darō.*

Katō: There's a general meeting of the labor union tomorrow. I wonder if everyone is supposed to attend.

Kanehara: We're busy now, so I think there is no need for
everyone to go.

この書類は人事課に提出するには及ばない。

*Kono shorui wa Jinjika ni teishutsu suru ni wa oyobanai.*

There is no reason for these documents to be submitted to
the Personnel Section.

## -Ppanashi ーっぱなし

| | |
|---|---|
| */-~~masu~~/ + ppanashi* | ／ー~~ます~~／＋っぱなし |
| *tachi/~~masu~~/ppanashi* | 立ち／~~ます~~／っぱなし |

This suffix is added after the */-masu/* stem to indicate that
an action has been begun but abandoned or forgotten in mid-
course or simply that an action is still continuing.

母親：窓が開けっぱなしよ。雨が降ってきたから閉めて
ちょうだい。[開ける *akeru*]

子供：はい。

*Hahaoya: Mado ga akeppanashi yo. Ame ga futte kita*
*kara shimete chōdai.*

*Kodomo: Hai.*

Mother: You left the window open. It's started raining, so
please shut it.

Child: Okay.

うちの子供はいつもおもちゃを出しっぱなしにするので、
困ります。[出す *dasu*]

*Uchi no kodomo wa itsumo omocha o dashippanashi ni*
*suru no de, komarimasu.*

I can't stand the way my kids always leave their toys out.

## Shiyō ga nai しようがない ━━━━━━━━━━

| | |
|---|---|
| noun + *no shiyō ga nai* | 名詞＋の＋しようがない |
| *setsume no shiyō ga nai* | 説明のしようがない |

This pattern indicates that there is no means, or way, of doing something. It follows a noun and the particle *no* の.

これは難しくて説明のしようがない。
*Kore wa muzukashikute setsumei no shiyō ga nai.*
This is so difficult there is no way of explaining it.

池田さんは大変気を悪くしているので、話のしようがな いんです。
*Ikeda-san wa taihen ki o waruku shite iru no de, hanashi no shiyō ga nai n' desu.*
Mr. Ikeda is in a very bad mood, so I wouldn't even bother trying to talk to him.

## Sae ... -ba さえ〜ーば ━━━━━━━━━━

| | |
|---|---|
| /~~-masu~~/ noun + *sae* + | ／ー~~ます~~／名詞＋さえ＋ |
| -*ba* form | ーば形 |
| *iki/~~masu~~/ sae sureba* | 行き／~~ます~~／さえすれば |

This pattern is similar to the English "if only this, then...." A verb's /-*masu*/ stem, a noun, or a pronoun precedes the particle *sae* さえ, which in turn precedes a verb in the conditional -*ba* form.

板倉：旅行の準備これでＯＫね。
宮川：あとは空港へ行きさえすればいいんだ。 [行く *iku*, する *suru*]
*Itakura: Ryokō no jumbi kore de ōkē ne.*
*Miyakawa: Ato wa kūkō e iki sae sureba ii n' da.*
Itakura: So all the preparations for the trip are okay, right?
Miyakawa: All that is left is to go to the airport.

塩田：この計画、あなたさえ賛成してくれればまとまる のよ。 [くれる *kureru*]

成沢：でもどうしても私は賛成できないの。

*Shioda: Kono keikaku, anata sae sansei shite kurereba matomaru no yo.*

*Narisawa: Demo dōshitemo watashi wa sansei dekinai no.*

Shioda: This plan can be carried out if you would just agree.

Narisawa (female): But just can't agree.

## Shika nai しかない

| | |
|---|---|
| plain form + *shika nai* | 原形 + しかない |
| *yaru shika nai* | やるしかない |

This pattern is an emphatic way of saying "only" or that there is only one course of action left. It follows the plain form of the verb.

いったん決めた以上やるしかない。

*Ittan kimeta ijō yaru shika nai.*

Once it's been decided, there's nothing left but to do it.

もう電車がないから、今から車で行くしかない。

*Mō densha ga nai kara, ima kara kuruma de iku shika nai.*

There are no more trains, so we'll just have to go by car.

## Ni shitagatte / ni tsurete にしたがって／につれて

| | |
|---|---|
| plain form + *ni shitagatte* | 原形 + にしたがって |
| *renshū suru ni shitagatte* | 練習するにしたがって |
| plain form + *ni tsurete* | 原形 + につれて |
| *kuraku naru ni tsurete* | 闇くなるにつれて |

These patterns, used after the plain form, correspond to the English "as" in "as one thing happens, something else happens, too." Of the two, *ni shitagatte* にしたがって tends to refer to cause and effect dependent on human will, while *ni tsurete* につれて tends to point to one natural phenomenon that leads to another. Nevertheless, the two expressions are often interchangeable.

サンチェス：漢字はなかなか憶えられませんね。
北原：毎日練習するにしたがって、憶えられますよ。

*Sanchesu: Kanji wa nakanaka oboeraremasen ne.*
*Kitahara: Mainichi renshū suru ni shitagatte, oboerare-*
*masu yo.*

Sanchez: Kanji are really hard to remember.
Kitahara: By practicing every day, you'll be able to remember them.

暗くなるにつれて、温度がだんだん下がっていった。
*Kuraku naru ni tsurete, ondo ga dandan sagatte itta.*
As it got darker, the temperature gradually fell.

## Ni suginai にすぎない

| plain form/-*ta*/noun + | 原形／一た／名詞＋に |
| *ni suginai* | すぎない |
| *tomaru*/ *tomatta*/ | 泊まる／泊まった／ |
| *ichipāsento ni suginai* | １パーセントにすぎない |

This phrase means "no more than" or "only." It is preceded by a plain form or informal past-tense verb or by a noun.

浅井：明日から旅行にいらっしゃるんですってね。
園田：旅行と言っても一晩泊まるにすぎないんですよ。

*Asai: Ashita kara ryokō ni irassharu n' desu 'tte ne.*
*Sonoda: Ryokō to itte mo hitoban tomaru ni suginai n'*
*desu yo.*

Asai: I hear you're leaving on a trip tomorrow.
Sonoda: It's not much of a trip. We'll only be gone one
night.

失業者が増えたと言っても、１パーセントにすぎない。
[増える *fueru*]
*Shitsugyō-sha ga fueta to itte mo, ichi-pāsento ni suginai.*
Although the number of unemployed people has in-
creased, it's still no more than one percent.

# Tabi ni たびに

| | |
|---|---|
| plain form + *tabi ni* | 原形 + たびに |
| *iku tabi ni* | 行くたびに |

Used after the plain form, this phrase means "every time" or "whenever."

この町を訪ねるたびに、子供の頃を思い出す。
*Kono machi o tazuneru tabi ni, kodomo no koro o omoidasu.*
Every time I visit this town, I remember my childhood.

山中：このへんは、崖が多いですね。
佐々木：台風がくるたびに、崖崩れがあって危ないんですよ。
*Yamanaka: Kono hen wa, gake ga ōi desu ne.*
*Sasaki: Taifū ga kuru tabi ni, gakekuzure ga atte abunai n' desu yo.*
Yamanaka: This area has a lot of cliffs.
Sasaki: It's dangerous because there are landslides whenever a typhoon comes through.

# -Ta ka to omou to / -ta totan ーたかと思うと／ ーたとたん

| | |
|---|---|
| *-ta ka to omou to* | ーた + かと思うと |
| *nonda ka to omou to* | 飲んだかと思うと |
| *-ta totan* | ーた + とたん |
| *nonda totan* | 飲んだとたん |

These patterns mean "immediately after." They follow the informal past tense.

三浦：きのうの帰り、雨に降られたでしょう。
荒木：それが、家に着いたかと思うと降り出したのよ。
[着く *tsuku*]
*Miura: Kinō no kaeri, ame ni furareta deshō.*

*Araki: Sore ga, ie ni tsuita ka to omou to furidashita no yo.*

Miura: On your way home yesterday, you must have got rained on.

Araki: Actually, it started raining the very moment I reached home.

学校から帰って来たかと思うと、子供はもう出かけてしまった。[来る *kuru*]

*Gakkō kara kaette kita ka to omou to, kodomo wa mō dekakete shimatta.*

No sooner had the kids got back from school than they went out again.

ロケットは飛び立ったとたんに見えなくなった。[飛び立つ *tobitatsu*]

*Roketto wa tobitatta totan ni mienaku natta.*

The rocket disappeared from sight almost the minute it blasted off.

## -Tara kaette ーたらかえって

| | |
|---|---|
| *-tara kaette* | ーたら + かえって |
| *tabetara kaette* | 食べたらかえって |

This construction indicates that the result of an action was the opposite of what was expected. The pattern consists of the *-tara* form of the verb followed by *kaette* かえって.

この薬を飲んだらかえってお腹が痛くなった。[飲む *nomu*]

*Kono kusuri o nondara kaette onaka ga itaku natta.*

I took this medicine, but it gave me a stomachache instead of making me feel better.

タクシーに乗ったらかえって遅くなった。[乗る *noru*]

*Takushī ni nottara kaette osoku natta.*

Although we took a taxi, we arrived later than we would have otherwise.

## -Te wa irarenai ーてはいられない

| | |
|---|---|
| *-te wa irarenai* | ーて＋はいられない |
| *jitto shite wa irarenai* | じっとしてはいられない |

This pattern means that one cannot continue a certain action because of nervousness or because one should be doing something else to respond to the demands of the moment. The *-te* form is followed by *wa irarenai* はいられない.

梶：もうすぐお客様がお着きになりますよ。
峯本：大変だ。のんびりお茶など飲んではいられない。
　　　[飲む *nomu*]

*Kaji: Mō sugu o-kyaku-sama ga o-tsuki ni narimasu yo.*
*Minemoto: Taihen da. Nombiri o-cha nado nonde wa
　　irarenai.*

Kaji: The guests are going to arrive pretty soon.
Minemoto: Oh, no! We can't just sit around like this
　　drinking tea.

あと５分ほどで合格者の発表があるので、受験生はじっ
としてはいられないだろう。[する *suru*]

*Ato gofun hodo de gōkaku-sha no happyō ga aru no de,
juken-sei wa jitto shite wa irarenai darō.*

Since the names of those who have passed will be announced in about five minutes, the students who took the test must be on pins and needles.

## -Te tamaranai ーてたまらない

| | |
|---|---|
| *-te tamaranai* | ーて＋たまらない |
| *nemukute tamaranai* | 眠くてたまらない |

This form is used to say that a person finds a certain condition or urge unbearable. The *-te* form of verbs or adjectives is followed by *tamaranai* たまらない.

和子：暑いわね。
沙織：喉が乾いてたまらない。[乾く *kawaku*]

和子：私も。冷たい水が飲みたくてたまらないわ。[飲む *nomu*]

*Kazuko: Atsui wa ne.*

*Saori: Nodo ga kawaite tamaranai.*

*Kazuko: Watashi mo. Tsumetai mizu ga nomitakute tamaranai wa.*

Kazuko (female): It's scorching.

Saori (female): My throat's so dry I can hardly stand it.

Kazuko: Me, too. I'm dying for a drink of cold water.

## -Te hajimete 　ーて初めて

| *-te hajimete* | ーて＋初めて |
|---|---|
| *kiite hajimete* | 聞いて初めて |

This pattern says that one action occurs for the first time because of another action. The *-te* form is followed by *hajimete* 初めて.

自分が子供を持って、初めて親のありがたみがわかる。[持つ *motte*]

*Jibun ga kodomo o motte, hajimete oya no arigatami ga wakaru.*

You feel truly grateful to your parents only after you have children of your own.

朝目がさめて初めて、外が雪なのに気がついた。[さめる *sameru*]

*Asa me ga samete hajimete, soto ga yuki na no ni ki ga tsuita.*

He noticed that there was snow outside only after he woke up in the morning.

## -Te bakari wa irarenai 　ーてばかりはいられない

| *-te bakari wa irarenai* | ーて＋ばかりはいられない |
|---|---|
| *nonde bakari wa irarenai* | 飲んでばかりはいられない |

This pattern is nearly the same as *-te wa irarenai* —ては
いられない, which appears on page 143. The word *bakari* ば
かり, meaning "only" or "nothing but," reinforces the notion
that one is doing something that should not be done.

早川：試験、もうすぐでしょう。

水野：そうなの。遊んでばかりはいられないのよ。［遊ぶ
　　*asobu*］

*Hayakawa: Shiken, mō sugu deshō.*

*Mizuno: Sō na no. Asonde bakari wa irarenai no yo.*

Hayakawa: The test is pretty soon, isn't it?

Mizuno (female): Yes, it is. I can't afford to be fooling
　　around.

お金が無いので、むだな物を買ってばかりはいられない。
　　［買う *kau*］

*O-kane ga nai no de, muda na mono o katte bakari wa
　　irarenai.*

I don't have any money, so I can't afford to buy things I
　　don't need.

## -Te mo ... -te mo —ても ～—ても

| *-te mo ... -te mo* | —て＋も＋～—て＋も |
|---|---|
| *benkyō shite mo benkyō shite mo* | 勉強しても勉強しても |

In this pattern, the same verb appears twice in the *-te*
form. The meaning is "no matter how much one does something, it is not enough."

吉田：論文できましたか。

荒井：それが、書いても書いてもうまくいかないんです。
　　［書く *kaku*］

*Yoshida: Rombun dekimashita ka.*

*Arai: Sore ga, kaite mo kaite mo umaku ikanai n' desu.*

Yoshida: Did you finish your thesis?

Arai: The thing is, I keep writing and writing, but it just
　　doesn't turn out the way it should.

働いても働いてもお金がたまらない。［働く *hataraku*］

*Hataraite mo hataraite mo o-kane ga tamaranai.*
No matter how hard I work, I can't save any money.

## O tsūjite を通じて

| | |
|---|---|
| noun + *o tsūjite* | 名詞 + を通じて |
| *ichinen o tsūjite* | 一年を通じて |

This phrase follows nouns and means "by means of," "through," or "throughout."

多田：林田さんをご存じですか。
宮本：ええ、相原さんを通じて一度お会いしたことがあるんですよ。
*Tada: Hayashida-san o go-zonji desu ka.*
*Miyamoto: Ē, Aihara-san o tsūjite ichido o-ai shita koto ga aru n' desu yo.*
Tada: Do you know Mr. Hayashida?
Miyamoto: Yes, I met him once through Ms. Aihara.

この辺は一年を通じて、気候が温和です。
*Kono hen wa ichinen o tsūjite, kikō ga onwa desu.*
The climate in this area is mild throughout the year.

## Yō ni ように

| | |
|---|---|
| affirmative/negative plain form + *yō ni* | 肯定／否定原形 + ように |
| *wakaru yō ni* | 分かるように |
| *wasurenai yō ni* | 忘れないように |

This form is used in mild imperatives. It follows the plain form of the verb in either the affirmative or the negative.

車を運転するときには、事故を起こさないように気をつけてください。 [起こす *okosu*]
*Kuruma o unten suru toki ni wa, jiko o okosanai yō ni ki o tsukete kudasai.*
When you drive, be careful not to cause any accidents.

駆け込み乗車をしないようにお願いします。 [する *suru*]
*Kakekomi jōsha o shinai yō ni onegai shimasu.*
Please do not rush to board trains.

## -Yō to mo -nai ーようとも ーない

| *-yō to mo -nai* | ーよう＋とも＋ーない |
|---|---|
| *iō to mo kikanai* | 言おうとも聞かない |

This pattern means "no matter how much something is done, it does not lead to another action that might ordinarily be expected." It consists of the informal volitional form of a verb (see page 57) followed by a negative form of another.

あの人は誰が何と言おうとも、決して聞かない。[言う *iu*]
*Ano hito wa dare ga nan to iō to mo, keshite kikanai.*
No matter what you say to her, she never listens.

どこへ行こうとも、故郷のことは忘れない。 [行く *iku*]
*Doko e ikō to mo, kokyō no koto wa wasurenai.*
No matter where I go, I can never forget my hometown.

## -Yō to ... mai to ーようと ～まいと

| *-yō to* + plain form + *mai to* | ーよう＋と＋原形＋まいと |
|---|---|
| *tabeyō to taberu mai to* | 食べようと食べるまいと |

This pattern means "(regardless of) whether or not...." As in the previous pattern, the verb appears first in the informal volitional form followed by *to* と. Then it appears again in the plain form before the negative particle *mai* まい.

他の人が行こうと行くまいと、私は行くつもりだ。
*Hoka no hito ga ikō to iku mai to, watashi wa iku tsumori da.*
I intend to go whether other people go or not.

吉田さんがいいと言おうと言うまいと、いっこう気にならない。

*Yoshida-san ga ii to iō to iu mai to, ikkō ki ni naranai.*
I don't care at all whether Ms. Yoshida says it's okay or not.

## Ya ina ya やいなや

| | |
|---|---|
| plain form + *ya ina ya* | 原形 + やいなや |
| *dekakeru ya ina ya* | 出かけるやいなや |

This somewhat literary expression means "as soon as" or "immediately after." It follows the plain form of the verb.

空が暗くなるやいなや、雨が降り出した。
*Sora ga kuraku naru ya ina ya, ame ga furidashita.*
No sooner had the sky turned dark than rain began to fall.

電車が止まるやいなや、満員の乗客が外にあふれ出た。
*Densha ga tomaru ya ina ya, man'in no jōkyaku ga soto ni afuredeta.*
No sooner had the jam-packed train come to a stop than the passengers began to spill out of it.

## -Zaru o enai ーざるをえない

| | |
|---|---|
| /-~~nai~~/ + *zaru o enai* | ／ー~~ない~~／ + ざるをえない |
| *ika/~~nai~~/zaru o enai* | 行か／~~ない~~／ざるをえない |

This is a literary expression meaning "must." The negative suffix *-zaru* ーざる replaces the final *-nai* ーない in the informal negative form of the verb. For example, *kaenai* 変えない becomes *kaezaru* 変えざる. The irregular verbs *kuru* 来る and *suru* する become *kozaru* 来ざる and *sezaru* せざる, respectively.

将来、この法律は変えざるをえなくなる。[変える *kaeru*]
*Shōrai, kono hōritsu wa kaezaru o enaku naru.*
It will become necessary to change this law in the future.

会社の創立記念のパーティだから、出席せざるをえない
だろう。[する *suru*]

*Kaisha no sōritsu kinen no pāti da kara, shusseki sezaru o enai darō.*

The party is in honor of the company's founding, so we have no choice but to attend.

# -Zu ni ーずに

---

| | |
|---|---|
| /-~~nai~~/ + *zu ni* | ／ー~~ない~~／ + ずに |
| *yoma/~~nai~~/zu ni* | 読ま／~~ない~~／ずに |

---

This form means "without doing ...," and it has the same meaning as the negative suffix *-nai* ーない followed by *de* で, as in 食べないで "without eating." The suffix *-zu* ーず replaces *-nai* ーない in the informal negative, so *tabenai* 食べない becomes *tabezu* 食べず. The irregular verbs *kuru* 来る and *suru* する become *kozu* 来ず and *sezu* せず.

神田：朝ご飯食べてきた？
渋谷：朝寝坊したから、今朝は食べずにきた。[食べる *taberu*]
*Kanda: Asa-gohan tabete kita?*
*Shibuya: Asa-nebō shita kara, kesa wa tabezu ni kita.*
Kanda: Did you eat breakfast before you came?
Shibuya: I slept late, so I came without eating.

先生は何も言わずに教室を出て行かれた。 [言う *iū*]
*Sensei wa nani mo iwazu ni kyōshitsu o dete ikareta.*
The teacher left the classroom without saying a word.

# Appendix: Verb Conjugations

## Group 1

| plain form | *-masu* form | *-te* form | *-nai* form | *-ta* form | *-ba* form |
|---|---|---|---|---|---|
| *agaru*<br>上がる<br>rise, go up | *agarimasu*<br>上がります | *agatte*<br>上がって | *agaranai*<br>上がらない | *agatta*<br>上がった | *agareba*<br>上がれば |
| *aku*<br>開く<br>open (i) | *akimasu*<br>開きます | *aite*<br>開いて | *akanai*<br>開かない | *aita*<br>開いた | *akeba*<br>開けば |
| *arau*<br>洗う<br>wash | *araimasu*<br>洗います | *aratte*<br>洗って | *arawanai*<br>洗わない | *aratta*<br>洗った | *araeba*<br>洗えば |
| *aru*<br>ある<br>exist | *arimasu*<br>あります | *atte*<br>あって | *nai*<br>ない | *atta*<br>あった | *areba*<br>あれば |
| *aruku*<br>歩く<br>walk | *arukimasu*<br>歩きます | *aruite*<br>歩いて | *arukanai*<br>歩かない | *aruita*<br>歩いた | *arukeba*<br>歩けば |
| *asobu*<br>遊ぶ<br>play | *asobimasu*<br>遊びます | *asonde*<br>遊んで | *asobanai*<br>遊ばない | *asonda*<br>遊んだ | *asobeba*<br>遊べば |
| *atsumaru*<br>集まる<br>get together (i) | *atsumarimasu*<br>集まります | *atsumatte*<br>集まって | *atsumaranai*<br>集まらない | *atsumatta*<br>集まった | *atsumareba*<br>集まれば |
| *au*<br>会う<br>meet | *aimasu*<br>会います | *atte*<br>会って | *awanai*<br>会わない | *atta*<br>会った | *aeba*<br>会えば |
| *azukaru*<br>預かる<br>deposit | *azukarimasu*<br>預かります | *azukatte*<br>預かって | *azukaranai*<br>預からない | *azukatta*<br>預かった | *azukareba*<br>預かれば |
| *dasu*<br>出す<br>take out, put out (t) | *dashimasu*<br>出します | *dashite*<br>出して | *dasanai*<br>出さない | *dashita*<br>出した | *daseba*<br>出せば |
| *erabu*<br>選ぶ<br>choose | *erabimasu*<br>選びます | *erande*<br>選んで | *erabanai*<br>選ばない | *eranda*<br>選んだ | *erabeba*<br>選べば |

| conditional | potential | volitional | passive | causative |
|---|---|---|---|---|
| *agattara*<br>上ったら | *agareru*<br>上がれる | *agarō*<br>上がろう | *agarareru*<br>上がられる | *agaraseru*<br>上がらせる |
| *aitara*<br>開いたら | —<br>— | *akō*<br>開こう | —<br>— | —<br>— |
| *arattara*<br>洗ったら | *araeru*<br>洗える | *araō*<br>洗おう | *arawareru*<br>洗われる | *arawaseru*<br>洗わせる |
| *attara*<br>あったら | —<br>— | *arō*<br>あろう | —<br>— | —<br>— |
| *aruitara*<br>歩いたら | *arukeru*<br>歩ける | *arukō*<br>歩こう | *arukareru*<br>歩かれる | *arukaseru*<br>歩かせる |
| *asondara*<br>遊んだら | *asoberu*<br>遊べる | *asobō*<br>遊ぼう | *asobareru*<br>遊ばれる | *asobaseru*<br>遊ばせる |
| *atsumattara*<br>集まったら | *atsumareru*<br>集まれる | *atsumarō*<br>集まろう | *atsumareru*<br>集まれる | *atsumaraseru*<br>集まらせる |
| *attara*<br>会ったら | *aeru*<br>会える | *aō*<br>会おう | *awareru*<br>会われる | *awaseru*<br>会わせる |
| *azukattara*<br>預かったら | *azukareru*<br>預かれる | *azukarō*<br>預かろう | *azukarareru*<br>預かられる | *azukaraseru*<br>預からせる |
| *dashitara*<br>出したら | *daseru*<br>出せる | *dasō*<br>出そう | *dasareru*<br>出される | *dasaseru*<br>出させる |
| *erandara*<br>選んだら | *eraberu*<br>選べる | *erabō*<br>選ぼう | *erabareru*<br>選ばれる | *erabaseru*<br>選ばせる |

| plain form | -masu form | -te form | -nai form | -ta form | -ba form |
|---|---|---|---|---|---|
| fumu<br>踏む<br>step on | fumimasu<br>踏みます | funde<br>踏んで | fumanai<br>踏まない | funda<br>踏んだ | fumeba<br>踏めば |
| furu<br>降る<br>rain, snow | furimasu<br>降ります | futte<br>降って | furanai<br>降らない | futta<br>降った | fureba<br>降れば |
| fuyasu<br>増やす<br>increase (t) | fuyashimasu<br>増やします | fuyashite<br>増やして | fuyasanai<br>増やさない | fuyashita<br>増やした | fuyaseba<br>増やせば |
| gambaru<br>頑張る<br>try hard | gambarimasu<br>頑張ります | gambatte<br>頑張って | gambaranai<br>頑張らない | gambatta<br>頑張った | gambareba<br>頑張れば |
| hairu<br>入る<br>enter (i) | hairimasu<br>入ります | haitte<br>入って | hairanai<br>入らない | haitta<br>入った | haireba<br>入れば |
| hajimaru<br>始まる<br>start (i) | hajimarimasu<br>始まります | hajimatte<br>始まって | hajimaranai<br>始まらない | hajimatta<br>始まった | hajimareba<br>始まれば |
| herasu<br>減らす<br>decrease (t) | herashimasu<br>減らします | herashite<br>減らして | herasanai<br>減らさない | herashita<br>減らした | heraseba<br>減らせば |
| heru<br>減る<br>decrease (i) | herimasu<br>減ります | hette<br>減って | heranai<br>減らない | hetta<br>減った | hereba<br>減れば |
| hiku<br>引く<br>pull | hikimasu<br>引きます | hiite<br>引いて | hikanai<br>引かない | hiita<br>引いた | hikeba<br>引けば |
| iku<br>行く<br>go | ikimasu<br>行きます | itte<br>行って | ikanai<br>行かない | itta<br>行った | ikeba<br>行けば |
| isogu<br>急ぐ<br>hurry | isogimasu<br>急ぎます | isoide<br>急いで | isoganai<br>急がない | isoida<br>急いだ | isogeba<br>急げば |
| iu (yū)<br>言う<br>say | iimasu<br>言います | itte (yutte)<br>言って | iwanai<br>言わない | itta (yutta)<br>言った | ieba<br>言えば |
| kaeru<br>帰る<br>return | kaerimasu<br>帰ります | kaette<br>帰って | kaeranai<br>帰らない | kaetta<br>帰った | kaereba<br>帰れば |

| conditional | potential | volitional | passive | causative |
| --- | --- | --- | --- | --- |
| *fundara*<br>踏んだら | *fumeru*<br>踏める | *fumō*<br>踏もう | *fumareru*<br>踏まれる | *fumaseru*<br>踏ませる |
| *futtara*<br>降ったら | —<br>— | *furō*<br>降ろう | *furareru*<br>降られる | *furaseru*<br>降らせる |
| *fuyashitara*<br>増やしたら | *fuyaseru*<br>増やせる | *fuyasō*<br>増やそう | *fuyasareru*<br>増やされる | *fuyasaseru*<br>増やさせる |
| *gambattara*<br>頑張ったら | *gambareru*<br>頑張れる | *gambarō*<br>頑張ろう | *gambarareru*<br>頑張られる | *gambaraseru*<br>頑張らせる |
| *haittara*<br>入ったら | *haireru*<br>入れる | *hairō*<br>入ろう | *hairareru*<br>入られる | *hairaseru*<br>入らせる |
| *hajimattara*<br>始まったら | —<br>— | *hajimarō*<br>始まろう | —<br>— | —<br>— |
| *herashitara*<br>減らしたら | *heraseru*<br>減らせる | *herasō*<br>減らそう | *herasareru*<br>減らされる | *herasaseru*<br>減らさせる |
| *hettara*<br>減ったら | —<br>— | *herō*<br>減ろう | —<br>— | —<br>— |
| *hiitara*<br>引いたら | *hikeru*<br>引ける | *hikō*<br>引こう | *hikareru*<br>引かれる | *hikaseru*<br>引かせる |
| *ittara*<br>行ったら | *ikeru*<br>行ける | *ikō*<br>行こう | *ikareru*<br>行かれる | *ikaseru*<br>行かせる |
| *isoidara*<br>急いだら | *isogeru*<br>急げる | *isogō*<br>急ごう | *isogareru*<br>急がれる | *isogaseru*<br>急がせる |
| *ittara (yuttara)*<br>言ったら | *ieru*<br>言える | *iō*<br>言おう | *iwareru*<br>言われる | *iwaseru*<br>言わせる |
| *kaettara*<br>帰ったら | *kaerareru*<br>帰られる | *kaerō*<br>帰ろう | *kaerareru*<br>帰られる | *kaeraseru*<br>帰らせる |

| plain form | -masu form | -te form | -nai form | -ta form | -ba form |
| --- | --- | --- | --- | --- | --- |
| *kakaru*<br>かかる<br>take (money, time) | *kakarimasu*<br>かかります | *kakatte*<br>かかって | *kakaranai*<br>かからない | *kakatta*<br>かかった | *kakareba*<br>かかれば |
| *kaku*<br>描く, 書く<br>draw, write | *kakimasu*<br>書きます | *kaite*<br>書いて | *kakanai*<br>書かない | *kaita*<br>書いた | *kakeba*<br>書けば |
| *kasu*<br>貸す<br>lend | *kashimasu*<br>貸します | *kashite*<br>貸して | *kasanai*<br>貸さない | *kashita*<br>貸した | *kaseba*<br>貸せば |
| *kau*<br>買う<br>buy | *kaimasu*<br>買います | *katte*<br>買って | *kawanai*<br>買わない | *katta*<br>買った | *kaeba*<br>買えば |
| *kawakasu*<br>乾かす<br>dry (t) | *kawakashimasu*<br>乾かします | *kawakashite*<br>乾かして | *kawakasanai*<br>乾かさない | *kawakashita*<br>乾かした | *kawakaseba*<br>乾かせば |
| *kawaku*<br>乾く<br>dry (i) | *kawakimasu*<br>乾きます | *kawaite*<br>乾いて | *kawakasanai*<br>乾かない | *kawaita*<br>乾いた | *kawakeba*<br>乾けば |
| *kazaru*<br>飾る<br>decorate | *kazarimasu*<br>飾ります | *kazatte*<br>飾って | *kazaranai*<br>飾らない | *kazatta*<br>飾った | *kazareba*<br>飾れば |
| *kesu*<br>消す<br>put out fire, turn off light (t) | *keshimasu*<br>消します | *keshite*<br>消して | *kesanai*<br>消さない | *keshita*<br>消した | *keseba*<br>消せば |
| *kiku*<br>聞く<br>listen | *kikimasu*<br>聞きます | *kiite*<br>聞いて | *kikanai*<br>聞かない | *kiita*<br>聞いた | *kikeba*<br>聞けば |
| *kimaru*<br>決まる<br>decide (i) | *kimarimasu*<br>決まります | *kimatte*<br>決って | *kimaranai*<br>決まらない | *kimatta*<br>決まった | *kimareba*<br>決まれば |
| *kiru*<br>切る<br>cut | *kirimasu*<br>切ります | *kitte*<br>切って | *kiranai*<br>切らない | *kitta*<br>切った | *kireba*<br>切れば |
| *kogu*<br>漕ぐ<br>row | *kogimasu*<br>漕ぎます | *koide*<br>漕いで | *koganai*<br>漕がない | *koida*<br>漕いだ | *kogeba*<br>漕げば |
| *komaru*<br>困る<br>be in trouble | *komarimasu*<br>困ります | *komatte*<br>困って | *komaranai*<br>困らない | *komatta*<br>困った | *komareba*<br>困れば |

| conditional | potential | volitional | passive | causative |
|---|---|---|---|---|
| *kakattara*<br>かかったら | —<br>— | *kakarō*<br>かかろう | | |
| *kaitara*<br>書いたら | *kakeru*<br>書ける | *kakō*<br>書こう | *kakareru*<br>書かれる | *kakaseru*<br>書かせる |
| *kashitara*<br>貸したら | *kaseru*<br>貸せる | *kasō*<br>貸そう | *kasareru*<br>貸される | *kasaseru*<br>貸させる |
| *kattara*<br>買ったら | *kaeru*<br>買える | *kaō*<br>買おう | *kawareru*<br>買われる | *kawaseru*<br>買わせる |
| *kawakashitara*<br>乾かしたら | *kawakaseru*<br>乾かせる | *kawakasō*<br>乾かそう | *kawakasareru*<br>乾かされる | *kawakasaseru*<br>乾かさせる |
| *kawaitara*<br>乾いたら | —<br>— | *kawakō*<br>乾こう | —<br>— | —<br>— |
| *kazattara*<br>飾ったら | *kazareru*<br>飾れる | *kazarō*<br>飾ろう | *kazarareru*<br>飾られる | *kazaraseru*<br>飾らせる |
| *keshitara*<br>消したら | *keseru*<br>消せる | *kesō*<br>消そう | *kesareru*<br>消される | *kesaseru*<br>消させる |
| *kiitara*<br>聞いたら | *kikeru*<br>聞ける | *kikō*<br>聞こう | *kikareru*<br>聞かれる | *kikaseru*<br>聞かせる |
| *kimattara*<br>決まったら | —<br>— | *kimarō*<br>決まろう | —<br>— | —<br>— |
| *kittara*<br>切ったら | *kireru*<br>切れる | *kirō*<br>切ろう | *kirareru*<br>切られる | *kiraseru*<br>切らせる |
| *koidara*<br>漕いだら | *kogeru*<br>漕げる | *kogō*<br>漕ごう | *kogareru*<br>漕がれる | *kogaseru*<br>漕がせる |
| *komattara*<br>困ったら | —<br>— | *komarō*<br>困ろう | —<br>— | *komaraseru*<br>困らせる |

| plain form | -masu form | -te form | -nai form | -ta form | -ba form |
|---|---|---|---|---|---|
| komu<br>混む<br>be crowded | komimasu<br>混みます | konde<br>混んで | komanai<br>混まない | konda<br>混んだ | komeba<br>混めば |
| korosu<br>殺す<br>kill | koroshimasu<br>殺します | koroshite<br>殺して | korosanai<br>殺さない | koroshita<br>殺した | koroseba<br>殺せば |
| maniau<br>間に合う<br>be on time, be enough | maniaimasu<br>間に合います | maniatte<br>間に合って | maniawanai<br>間に合わない | maniatta<br>間に合った | maniaeba<br>間に合えば |
| matsu<br>待つ<br>wait | machimasu<br>待ちます | matte<br>待って | matanai<br>待たない | matta<br>待った | mateba<br>待てば |
| mayou<br>迷う<br>be at a loss | mayoimasu<br>迷います | mayotte<br>迷って | mayowanai<br>迷わない | mayotta<br>迷った | mayoeba<br>迷えば |
| migaku<br>磨く<br>polish, brush, shine | migakimasu<br>磨きます | migaite<br>磨いて | migakanai<br>磨かない | migaita<br>磨いた | migakeba<br>磨けば |
| mitsukaru<br>見つかる<br>be found out (i) | mitsukarimasu<br>見つかります | mitsukatte<br>見つかって | mitsukaranai<br>見つからない | mitsukatta<br>見つかった | mitsukareba<br>見つかれば |
| morau<br>貰う<br>be given, receive | moraimasu<br>貰います | moratte<br>貰って | morawanai<br>貰わない | moratta<br>貰った | moraeba<br>貰えば |
| motsu<br>持つ<br>have, hold | mochimasu<br>持ちます | motte<br>持って | motanai<br>持たない | motta<br>持った | moteba<br>持てば |
| naku<br>泣く<br>cry | nakimasu<br>泣きます | naite<br>泣いて | nakanai<br>泣かない | naita<br>泣いた | nakeba<br>泣けば |
| nakunaru<br>なくなる<br>pass away, disappear | nakunarimasu<br>なくなります | nakunatte<br>なくなって | nakunaranai<br>なくならない | nakunatta<br>なくなった | nakunareba<br>なくなれば |
| naoru<br>直る<br>recover, be fixed (i) | naorimasu<br>直ります | naotte<br>直って | naoranai<br>直らない | naotta<br>直った | naoreba<br>直れば |
| naosu<br>直す<br>fix, mend (t) | naoshimasu<br>直します | naoshite<br>直して | naosanai<br>直さない | naoshita<br>直した | naoseba<br>直せば |

| conditional | potential | volitional | passive | causative |
|---|---|---|---|---|
| *kondara* 混んだら | — | *komō* 混もう | — | *komaseru* 混ませる |
| *koroshitara* 殺したら | *koroseru* 殺せる | *korosō* 殺そう | *korosareru* 殺される | *korosaseru* 殺させる |
| *maniattara* 間に合ったら | — | *maniaō* 間に合おう | — | *maniawaseru* 間に合わせる |
| *mattara* 待ったら | *materu* 待てる | *matō* 待とう | *matareru* 待たれる | *mataseru* 待たせる |
| *mayottara* 迷ったら | *mayoeru* 迷える | *mayoō* 迷おう | *mayowareru* 迷われる | *mayowaseru* 迷わせる |
| *migaitara* 磨いたら | *migakeru* 磨ける | *migakō* 磨こう | *migakareru* 磨かれる | *migakaseru* 磨かせる |
| *mitsukattara* 見つかったら | — | *mitsukarō* 見つかろう | — | — |
| *morattara* 貰ったら | *moraeru* 貰える | *moraō* 貰おう | *morawareru* 貰われる | *morawaseru* 貰わせる |
| *mottara* 持ったら | *moteru* 持てる | *motō* 持とう | *motareru* 持たれる | *motaseru* 持たせる |
| *naitara* 泣いたら | *nakeru* 泣ける | *nakō* 泣こう | *nakareru* 泣かれる | *nakaseru* 泣かせる |
| *nakunattara* なくなったら | — | *nakunarō* なくなろう | — | — |
| *naottara* 直ったら | *naoreru* 直れる | *naorō* 直ろう | *naorareru* 直られる | *naoraseru* 直らせる |
| *naoshitara* 直したら | *naoseru* 直せる | *naosō* 直そう | *naosareru* 直される | *naosaseru* 直させる |

| plain form | -masu form | -te form | -nai form | -ta form | -ba form |
|---|---|---|---|---|---|
| narabu 並ぶ stand in line (i) | narabimasu 並びます | narande 並んで | narabanai 並ばない | naranda 並んだ | narabeba 並べば |
| narau 習う learn | naraimasu 習います | naratte 習って | narawanai 習わない | naratta 習った | naraeba 習えば |
| naru なる become | narimasu なります | natte なって | naranai ならない | natta なった | nareba なれば |
| nokoru 残る remain (i) | nokorimasu 残ります | nokotte 残って | nokoranai 残らない | nokotta 残った | nokoreba 残れば |
| nokosu 残す leave, remain (t) | nokoshimasu 残します | nokoshite 残して | nokosanai 残さない | nokoshita 残した | nokoseba 残せば |
| nomu 飲む drink | nomimasu 飲みます | nonde 飲んで | nomanai 飲まない | nonda 飲んだ | nomeba 飲めば |
| noru 乗る get on | norimasu 乗ります | notte 乗って | noranai 乗らない | notta 乗った | noreba 乗れば |
| nusumu 盗む steal | nusumimasu 盗みます | nusunde 盗んで | nusumanai 盗まない | nusunda 盗んだ | nusumeba 盗めば |
| odoru 踊る dance | odorimasu 踊ります | odotte 踊って | odoranai 踊らない | odotta 踊った | odoreba 踊れば |
| okosu 起こす wake up (t) | okoshimasu 起こします | okoshite 起こして | okosanai 起こさない | okoshita 起こした | okoseba 起こせば |
| oku 置く put on | okimasu 置きます | oite 置いて | okanai 置かない | oita 置いた | okeba 置けば |
| okuru 送る send | okurimasu 送ります | okutte 送って | okuranai 送らない | okutta 送った | okureba 送れば |
| omou 思う think | omoimasu 思います | omotte 思って | omowanai 思わない | omotta 思った | omoeba 思えば |

| conditional | potential | volitional | passive | causative |
|---|---|---|---|---|
| narandara 並んだら | naraberu 並べる | narabō 並ぼう | narabareru 並ばれる | narabaseru 並ばせる |
| narattara 習ったら | naraeru 習える | naraō 習おう | narawareru 習われる | narawaseru 習わせる |
| nattara なったら | nareru なれる | narō なろう | narareru なられる | naraseru ならせる |
| nokottara 残ったら | nokoreru 残れる | nokorō 残ろう | nokorareru 残られる | nokoraseru 残らせる |
| nokoshitara 残したら | nokoseru 残せる | nokosō 残そう | nokosareru 残される | nokosaseru 残させる |
| nondara 飲んだら | nomeru 飲める | nomō 飲もう | nomareru 飲まれる | nomaseru 飲ませる |
| nottara 乗ったら | noreru 乗れる | norō 乗ろう | norareru 乗られる | noraseru 乗らせる |
| nusundara 盗んだら | nusumeru 盗める | nusumō 盗もう | nusumareru 盗まれる | nusumaseru 盗ませる |
| odottara 踊ったら | odoreru 踊れる | odorō 踊ろう | odorareru 踊られる | odoraseru 踊らせる |
| okoshitara 起こしたら | okoseru 起こせる | okosō 起こそう | okosareru 起こされる | okosaseru 起こさせる |
| oitara 置いたら | okeru 置ける | okō 置こう | okareru 置かれる | okaseru 置かせる |
| okuttara 送ったら | okureru 送れる | okurō 送ろう | okurareru 送られる | okuraseru 送らせる |
| omottara 思ったら | omoeru 思える | omoō 思おう | omowareru 思われる | omowaseru 思わせる |

| plain form | -masu form | -te form | -nai form | -ta form | -ba form |
|---|---|---|---|---|---|
| orosu 降ろす put down (t) | oroshimasu 降ろします | oroshite 降ろして | orosanai 降ろさない | oroshita 降ろした | oroseba 降ろせば |
| osu 押す push | oshimasu 押します | oshite 押して | osanai 押さない | oshita 押した | oseba 押せば |
| otosu 落とす drop (t) | otoshimasu 落とします | otoshite 落として | otosanai 落とさない | otoshita 落とした | otoseba 落とせば |
| owaru 終る finish | owarimasu 終わります | owatte 終わって | owaranai 終わらない | owatta 終わった | owareba 終われば |
| oyogu 泳ぐ swim | oyogimasu 泳ぎます | oyoide 泳いで | oyoganai 泳がない | oyoida 泳いだ | oyogeba 泳げば |
| sagaru 下がる go down, step back, retire | sagarimasu 下がります | sagatte 下がって | sagaranai 下がらない | sagatta 下がった | sagareba 下がれば |
| sagasu 探す look for | sagashimasu 探します | sagashite 探がして | sagasanai 探さない | sagashita 探した | sagaseba 探せば |
| saku 咲く bloom | sakimasu 咲きます | saite 咲いて | sakanai 咲かない | saita 咲いた | sakeba 咲けば |
| shimaru 閉まる close (i) | shimarimasu 閉まります | shimatte 閉まって | shimaranai 閉まらない | shimatta 閉まった | shimareba 閉まれば |
| shiru 知る know | shirimasu 知ります | shitte 知って | shiranai 知らない | shitta 知った | shireba 知れば |
| sugosu 過ごす pass (t) | sugoshimasu 過ごします | sugoshite 過ごして | sugosanai 過ごさない | sugoshita 過ごした | sugoseba 過ごせば |
| susumu 進む advance, go ahead | susumimasu 進みます | susunde 進んで | susumanai 進まない | susunda 進んだ | susumeba 進めば |
| suu 吸う smoke | suimasu 吸います | sutte 吸って | suwanai 吸わない | sutta 吸った | sueba 吸えば |

| conditional | potential | volitional | passive | causative |
|---|---|---|---|---|
| *oroshitara*<br>降ろしたら | *oroseru*<br>降ろせる | *orosō*<br>降ろそう | *orosareru*<br>降ろされる | *orosaseru*<br>降ろさせる |
| *oshitara*<br>押したら | *oseru*<br>押せる | *osō*<br>押そう | *osareru*<br>押される | *osaseru*<br>押させる |
| *otoshitara*<br>落としたら | *otoseru*<br>落とせる | *otosō*<br>落とそう | *otosareru*<br>落とされる | *otosaseru*<br>落とさせる |
| *owattara*<br>終わったら | *owareru*<br>終われる | *owarasō*<br>終わらそう | *owarareru*<br>終わられる | *owaraseru*<br>終わらせる |
| *oyoidara*<br>泳いだら | *oyogeru*<br>泳げる | *oyogō*<br>泳ごう | *oyogareru*<br>泳がれる | *oyogaseru*<br>泳がせる |
| *sagattara*<br>下がったら | *sagareru*<br>下がれる | *sagarō*<br>下がろう | *sagarareru*<br>下がられる | *sagaraseru*<br>下がらせる |
| *sagashitara*<br>探したら | *sagaseru*<br>探せる | *sagasō*<br>探そう | *sagasareru*<br>探される | *sagasaseru*<br>探させる |
| *saitara*<br>咲いたら | *sakeru*<br>咲ける | *sakō*<br>咲こう | *sakareru*<br>咲かれる | *sakaseru*<br>咲かせる |
| *shimattara*<br>閉まったら | — | *shimarō*<br>閉まろう | — | — |
| *shittara*<br>知ったら | *shireru*<br>知れる | *shirō*<br>知ろう | *shirareru*<br>知られる | *shiraseru*<br>知らせる |
| *sugoshitara*<br>過ごしたら | *sugoseru*<br>過ごせる | *sugosō*<br>過ごそう | *sugosareru*<br>過ごされる | *sugosaseru*<br>過ごさせる |
| *susundara*<br>進んだら | *susumeru*<br>進める | *susumō*<br>進もう | *susumareru*<br>進まれる | *susumaseru*<br>進ませる |
| *suttara*<br>吸ったら | *sueru*<br>吸える | *suō*<br>吸おう | *suwareru*<br>吸われる | *suwaseru*<br>吸わせる |

| plain form | -masu form | -te form | -nai form | -ta form | -ba form |
|---|---|---|---|---|---|
| suwaru 座る sit down | suwarimasu 座ります | suwatte 座って | suwaranai 座らない | suwatta 座った | suwareba 座れば |
| tatsu 立つ stand up | tachimasu 立ちます | tatte 立って | tatanai 立たない | tatta 立った | tateba 立てば |
| tomaru 止まる stop (i) | tomarimasu 止まります | tomatte 止まって | tomaranai 止まらない | tomatta 止まった | tomareba 止まれば |
| toru 取る pick up, take | torimasu 取ります | totte 取って | toranai 取らない | totta 取った | toreba 取れば |
| tsukau 使う use | tsukaimasu 使います | tsukatte 使って | tsukawanai 使わない | tsukatta 使った | tsukaeba 使えば |
| tsuku 着く arrive (i) | tsukimasu 着きます | tsuite 着いて | tsukanai 着かない | tsuita 着いた | tsukeba 着けば |
| tsukuru 作る make | tsukurimasu 作ります | tsukutte 作って | tsukuranai 作らない | tsukutta 作った | tsukureba 作れば |
| tsuzuku 続く go on (i) | tsuzukimasu 続きます | tsuzuite 続いて | tsuzukanai 続かない | tsuzuita 続いた | tsuzukeba 続けば |
| ugoku 動く move | ugokimasu 動きます | ugoite 動いて | ugokanai 動かない | ugoita 動いた | ugokeba 動けば |
| uru 売る sell | urimasu 売ります | utte 売って | uranai 売らない | utta 売った | ureba 売れば |
| utau 歌う sing | utaimasu 歌います | utatte 歌って | utawanai 歌わない | uttata 歌った | utaeba 歌えば |
| utsuru 移る move, change, transfer | utsurimasu 移ります | utsutte 移って | utsuranai 移らない | utsutta 移った | utsureba 移れば |
| wakaru 分かる understand | wakarimasu 分かります | wakatte 分かって | wakaranai 分からない | wakatta 分かった | wakareba 分かれば |

| conditional | potential | volitional | passive | causative |
| --- | --- | --- | --- | --- |
| *suwattara*<br>座ったら | *suwareru*<br>座われる | *suwarō*<br>座ろう | *suwarareru*<br>座られる | *suwaraseru*<br>座らせる |
| *tattara*<br>立ったら | *tateru*<br>立てる | *tatō*<br>立とう | *tatareru*<br>立たれる | *tataseru*<br>立たせる |
| *tomattara*<br>止まったら | *tomareru*<br>止まれる | *tomarō*<br>止まろう | *tomarareru*<br>止まられる | *tomaraseru*<br>止まらせる |
| *tottara*<br>取ったら | *toreru*<br>取れる | *torō*<br>取ろう | *torareru*<br>取られる | *toraseru*<br>取らせる |
| *tsukattara*<br>使ったら | *tsukaeru*<br>使える | *tsukaō*<br>使おう | *tsukawareru*<br>使われる | *tsukawaseru*<br>使わせる |
| *tsuitara*<br>着いたら | *tsukeru*<br>着ける | *tsukō*<br>着こう | *tsukareru*<br>着かれる | *tsukaseru*<br>着かせる |
| *tsukuttara*<br>作ったら | *tsukureru*<br>作れる | *tsukurō*<br>作ろう | *tsukurareru*<br>作られる | *tsukuraseru*<br>作らせる |
| *tsuzuitara*<br>続いたら | *tsuzukeru*<br>続ける | *tsuzukō*<br>続こう | *tsuzukareru*<br>続かれる | *tsuzukaseru*<br>続かせる |
| *ugoitara*<br>動いたら | *ugokeru*<br>動ける | *ugokō*<br>動こう | *ugokareru*<br>動かれる | *ugokaseru*<br>動かせる |
| *uttara*<br>売ったら | *ureru*<br>売れる | *urō*<br>売ろう | *urareru*<br>売られる | *uraseru*<br>売らせる |
| *utattara*<br>歌ったら | *utaeru*<br>歌える | *utaō*<br>歌おう | *utawareru*<br>歌われる | *utawaseru*<br>歌わせる |
| *utsuttara*<br>移ったら | *utsureru*<br>移れる | *utsurō*<br>移ろう | *utsurareru*<br>移られる | *utsuraseru*<br>移らせる |
| *wakattara*<br>分ったら | — | *wakarō*<br>分かろう | *wakarareru*<br>分かられる | *wakaraseru*<br>分からせる |

| plain form | -*masu* form | -*te* form | -*nai* form | -*ta* form | -*ba* form |
|---|---|---|---|---|---|
| *yamu*<br>止む<br>stop | *yamimasu*<br>止みます | *yande*<br>止んで | *yamanai*<br>止まない | *yanda*<br>止んだ | *yameba*<br>止めば |
| *yaru*<br>やる<br>do, give | *yarimasu*<br>やります | *yatte*<br>やって | *yaranai*<br>やらない | *yatta*<br>やった | *yareba*<br>やれば |
| *yasumu*<br>休む<br>rest | *yasumimasu*<br>休みます | *yasunde*<br>休んで | *yasumanai*<br>休まない | *yasunda*<br>休んだ | *yasumeba*<br>休めば |
| *yomu*<br>読む<br>read | *yomimasu*<br>読みます | *yonde*<br>読んで | *yomanai*<br>読まない | *yonda*<br>読んだ | *yomeba*<br>読めば |
| *yoru*<br>寄る<br>pass over, drop in | *yorimasu*<br>寄ります | *yotte*<br>寄って | *yoranai*<br>寄らない | *yotta*<br>寄った | *yoreba*<br>寄れば |

## Group 2

| plain form | -*masu* form | -*te* form | -*nai* form | -*ta* form | -*ba* form |
|---|---|---|---|---|---|
| *ageru*<br>上げる<br>give | *agemasu*<br>上げます | *agete*<br>上げて | *agenai*<br>上げない | *ageta*<br>上げた | *agereba*<br>上げれば |
| *akeru*<br>開ける<br>open (t) | *akemasu*<br>開けます | *akete*<br>開けて | *akenai*<br>開けない | *aketa*<br>開けた | *akereba*<br>開ければ |
| *arawareru*<br>現れる<br>appear (i) (表れる be expressed) | *arawaremasu*<br>現れます | *arawarete*<br>現れて | *arawarenai*<br>現れない | *arawareta*<br>現れた | *arawarereba*<br>現れれば |
| *deru*<br>出る<br>go out (i) | *demasu*<br>出ます | *dete*<br>出て | *denai*<br>出ない | *deta*<br>出た | *dereba*<br>出れば |
| *fueru*<br>増える<br>increase (i) | *fuemasu*<br>増えます | *fuete*<br>増えて | *fuenai*<br>増えない | *fueta*<br>増えた | *fuereba*<br>増えれば |
| *hajimeru*<br>始める<br>start, begin (t) | *hajimemasu*<br>始めます | *hajimete*<br>始めて | *hajimenai*<br>始めない | *hajimeta*<br>始めた | *hajimereba*<br>始めれば |

| conditional | potential | volitional | passive | causative |
|---|---|---|---|---|
| *yandara*<br>止んだら | — | *yamō*<br>止もう | — | |
| *yattara*<br>やったら | *yareru*<br>やれる | *yarō*<br>やろう | *yarareru*<br>やられる | |
| *yasundara*<br>休んだら | *yasumeru*<br>休める | *yasumō*<br>休もう | *yasumareru*<br>休まれる | *...aseru* |
| *yondara*<br>読んだら | *yomeru*<br>読める | *yomō*<br>読もう | *yomareru*<br>読まれる | *yomaseru*<br>読ませる |
| *yottara*<br>寄ったら | *yoreru*<br>寄れる | *yorō*<br>寄ろう | *yorareru*<br>寄られる | *yoraseru*<br>寄らせる |

| conditional | potential | volitional | passive | causative |
|---|---|---|---|---|
| *agetara*<br>上げたら | *agerareru*<br>上げられる | *ageyō*<br>上げよう | *agerareru*<br>上げられる | *agesaseru*<br>上げさせる |
| *aketara*<br>開けたら | *akerareru*<br>開けられる | *akeyō*<br>開けよう | *akerareru*<br>開けられる | *akesaseru*<br>開けさせる |
| *arawaretara*<br>現れたら | *arawarerareru*<br>現れられる | *arawareyō*<br>現れよう | *arawarerareru*<br>現れられる | *arawaresaseru*<br>現れさせる |
| *detara*<br>出たら | *derareru*<br>出られる | *deyō*<br>出よう | *derareru*<br>出られる | *desaseru*<br>出させる |
| *fuetara*<br>増えたら | *fuerareru*<br>増えられる | *fueyō*<br>増えよう | *fuerareru*<br>増えられる | *fuesaseru*<br>増えさせる |
| *hajimetara*<br>始めたら | *hajimerareru*<br>始められる | *hajimeyō*<br>始めよう | *hajimerareru*<br>始められる | *hajimesaseru*<br>始めさせる |

| plain form | -*masu* form | -*te* form | -*nai* form | -*ta* form | -*ba* form |
|---|---|---|---|---|---|
| *ireru*<br>入れる<br>put in (t) | *iremasu*<br>入れます | *irete*<br>入れて | *irenai*<br>入れない | *ireta*<br>入れた | *irereba*<br>入れれば |
| *kaeru*<br>変える<br>change | *kaemasu*<br>変えます | *kaete*<br>変えて | *kaenai*<br>変えない | *kaeta*<br>変えた | *kaereba*<br>変えれば |
| *kakeru*<br>かける<br>make a phone call, hang, spend time | *kakemasu*<br>かけます | *kakete*<br>かけて | *kakenai*<br>かけない | *kaketa*<br>かけた | *kakereba*<br>かければ |
| *kangaeru*<br>考える<br>think | *kangaemasu*<br>考えます | *kangaete*<br>考えて | *kangaenai*<br>考えない | *kangaeta*<br>考えた | *kangaereba*<br>考えれば |
| *kieru*<br>消える<br>put out, be turned off (i) | *kiemasu*<br>消えます | *kiete*<br>消えて | *kienai*<br>消えない | *kieta*<br>消えた | *kiereba*<br>消えれば |
| *kikoeru*<br>聞こえる<br>can be heard | *kikoemasu*<br>聞こえます | *kikoete*<br>聞こえて | *kikoenai*<br>聞こえない | *kikoeta*<br>聞こえた | *kikoereba*<br>聞こえれば |
| *kimeru*<br>決める<br>decide | *kimemasu*<br>決めます | *kimete*<br>決めて | *kimenai*<br>決めない | *kimeta*<br>決めた | *kimereba*<br>決めれば |
| *kireru*<br>切れる<br>be cut, stop (i) | *kiremasu*<br>切れます | *kirete*<br>切れて | *kirenai*<br>切れない | *kireta*<br>切れた | *kirereba*<br>切れれば |
| *kiru*<br>着る<br>put on | *kimasu*<br>着ます | *kite*<br>着て | *kinai*<br>着ない | *kita*<br>着た | *kireba*<br>着れば |
| *kowareru*<br>壊れる<br>break (i) | *kowaremasu*<br>壊れます | *kowarete*<br>壊れて | *kowarenai*<br>壊れない | *kowareta*<br>壊れた | *kowarereba*<br>壊れれば |
| *kureru*<br>くれる<br>be given | *kuremasu*<br>くれます | *kurete*<br>くれて | *kurenai*<br>くれない | *kureta*<br>くれた | *kurereba*<br>くれれば |
| *miru*<br>見る<br>see, look | *mimasu*<br>見ます | *mite*<br>見て | *minai*<br>見ない | *mita*<br>見た | *mireba*<br>見れば |
| *mukaeru*<br>迎える<br>welcome, receive | *mukaemasu*<br>迎えます | *mukaete*<br>迎えて | *mukaenai*<br>迎えない | *mukaeta*<br>迎えた | *mukaereba*<br>迎えれば |

| conditional | potential | volitional | passive | causative |
|---|---|---|---|---|
| *iretara*<br>入れたら | *irerareru*<br>入れられる | *ireyō*<br>入れよう | *irerareru*<br>入れられる | *iresaseru*<br>入れさせる |
| *kaetara*<br>変えたら | *kaerareru*<br>変えられる | *kaeyō*<br>変えよう | *kaerareru*<br>変えられる | *kaesaseru*<br>変えさせる |
| *kaketara*<br>かけたら | *kakerareru*<br>かけられる | *kakeyō*<br>かけよう | *kakerareru*<br>かけられる | *kakesaseru*<br>かけさせる |
| *kangaetara*<br>考えたら | *kangaerareru*<br>考えられる | *kangaeyō*<br>考えよう | *kangaerareru*<br>考えられる | *kangaesaseru*<br>考えさせる |
| *kietara*<br>消えたら | *kierareru*<br>消えられる | *kieyō*<br>消えよう | *kierareru*<br>消えられる | *kiesaseru*<br>消えさせる |
| *kikoetara*<br>聞こえたら | —<br>— | *kikoeyō*<br>聞こえよう | —<br>— | —<br>— |
| *kimetara*<br>決めたら | *kimerareru*<br>決められる | *kimeyō*<br>決めよう | *kimerareru*<br>決められる | *kimesaseru*<br>決めさせる |
| *kiretara*<br>切れたら | —<br>— | *kireyō*<br>切れよう | —<br>— | —<br>— |
| *kitara*<br>着たら | *kirareru*<br>着られる | *kiyō*<br>着よう | *kirareru*<br>着られる | *kisaseru*<br>着させる |
| *kowaretara*<br>壊れたら | —<br>— | *kowareyō*<br>壊れよう | —<br>— | —<br>— |
| *kuretara*<br>くれたら | *kurerareru*<br>くれられる | *kureyō*<br>くれよう | *kurerareru*<br>くれられる | *kuresaseru*<br>くれさせる |
| *mitara*<br>見たら | *mirareru*<br>見られる | *miyō*<br>見よう | *mirareru*<br>見られる | *miraseru*<br>見らせる |
| *mukaetara*<br>迎えたら | *mukaerareru*<br>迎えられる | *mukaeyō*<br>迎えよう | *mukaerareru*<br>迎えられる | *mukaesaseru*<br>迎えさせる |

| plain form | -masu form | -te form | -nai form | -ta form | -ba form |
|---|---|---|---|---|---|
| naraberu<br>並べる | narabemasu<br>並べます | narabete<br>並べて | narabenai<br>並べない | narabeta<br>並べた | narabereba<br>並べれば |
| put things in row, arrange, put things in order (t) | | | | | |
| nareru<br>慣れる | naremasu<br>慣れます | narete<br>慣れて | narenai<br>慣れない | nareta<br>慣れた | narereba<br>慣れれば |
| get used to | | | | | |
| neru<br>寝る | nemasu<br>寝ます | nete<br>寝て | nenai<br>寝ない | neta<br>寝た | nereba<br>寝れば |
| sleep | | | | | |
| niru<br>似る | nimasu<br>似ます | nite<br>似て | ninai<br>似ない | nita<br>似た | nireba<br>似れば |
| resemble, look like | | | | | |
| norikaeru<br>乗り換える | norikaemasu<br>乗り換えます | norikaete<br>乗り換えて | norikaenai<br>乗り換えない | norikaeta<br>乗り換えた | norikaereba<br>乗り換えれば |
| transfer (a train, bus, etc.) | | | | | |
| noseru<br>乗せる | nosemasu<br>乗せます | nosete<br>乗せて | nosenai<br>乗せない | noseta<br>乗せた | nosereba<br>乗せれば |
| put something on, place on the top of (t) | | | | | |
| ochiru<br>落ちる | ochimasu<br>落ちます | ochite<br>落ちて | ochinai<br>落ちない | ochita<br>落ちた | ochireba<br>落ちれば |
| fall, drop (i) | | | | | |
| oeru<br>終える | oemasu<br>終えます | oete<br>終えて | oenai<br>終えない | oeta<br>終えた | oereba<br>終えれば |
| finish, end (t) | | | | | |
| okiru<br>起きる | okimasu<br>起きます | okite<br>起きて | okinai<br>起きない | okita<br>起きた | okireba<br>起きれば |
| get up (i) | | | | | |
| oriru<br>降りる | orimasu<br>降ります | orite<br>降りて | orinai<br>降りない | orita<br>降りた | orireba<br>降りれば |
| get off (i) | | | | | |
| oshieru<br>教える | oshiemasu<br>教えます | oshiete<br>教えて | oshienai<br>教えない | oshieta<br>教えた | oshiereba<br>教えれば |
| teach | | | | | |
| shimeru<br>閉める | shimemasu<br>閉めます | shimete<br>閉めて | shimenai<br>閉めない | shimeta<br>閉めた | shimereba<br>閉めれば |
| close, shut (t) | | | | | |
| shiraberu<br>調べる | shirabemasu<br>調べます | shirabete<br>調べて | shirabenai<br>調べない | shirabeta<br>調べた | shirabereba<br>調べれば |
| check, examine | | | | | |

| conditional | potential | volitional | passive | causative |
|---|---|---|---|---|
| *narabetara*<br>並べたら | *naraberareru*<br>並べられる | *narabeyō*<br>並べよう | *naraberareru*<br>並べられる | *narabesaseru*<br>並べさせる |
| *naretara*<br>慣れたら | *narerareru*<br>慣れられる | *nareyō*<br>慣れよう | *narerareru*<br>慣れられる | *naresaseru*<br>慣れさせる |
| *netara*<br>寝たら | *nerareru*<br>寝られる | *neyō*<br>寝よう | *nerareru*<br>寝られる | *nesaseru*<br>寝させる |
| *nitara*<br>似たら | *nirareru*<br>似られる | *niyō*<br>似よう | *nirareru*<br>似られる | *nisaseru*<br>似させる |
| *norikaetara*<br>乗り換えたら | *norikaerareru*<br>乗り換えられる | *norikaeyō*<br>乗り換えよう | *norikaerareru*<br>乗り換えられる | *norikaesaseru*<br>乗り換えさせる |
| *nosetara*<br>乗せたら | *noserareru*<br>乗せられる | *noseyō*<br>乗せよう | *noserareru*<br>乗せられる | *nosesaseru*<br>乗せさせる |
| *ochitara*<br>落ちたら | *ochirareru*<br>落ちられる | *ochiyō*<br>落ちよう | *ochirareru*<br>落ちられる | *ochiraseru*<br>落ちらせる |
| *oetara*<br>終えたら | *oerareru*<br>終えられる | *oeyō*<br>終えよう | *oerareru*<br>終えられる | *oesaseru*<br>終えさせる |
| *okitara*<br>起きたら | *okirareru*<br>起きられる | *okiyō*<br>起きよう | *okirareru*<br>起きられる | *okisaseru*<br>起きさせる |
| *oritara*<br>降りたら | *orirareru*<br>降りられる | *oriyō*<br>降りよう | *orirareru*<br>降りられる | *orisaseru*<br>降りさせる |
| *oshietara*<br>教えたら | *oshierareru*<br>教えられる | *oshieyō*<br>教えよう | *oshierareru*<br>教えられる | *oshiesaseru*<br>教えさせる |
| *shimetara*<br>閉めたら | *shimerareru*<br>閉められる | *shimeyō*<br>閉めよう | *shimerareru*<br>閉められる | *shimesaseru*<br>閉めさせる |
| *shirabetara*<br>調べたら | *shiraberareru*<br>調べられる | *shirabeyō*<br>調べよう | *shiraberareru*<br>調べられる | *shirabesaseru*<br>調べさせる |

| plain form | -*masu* form | -*te* form | -*nai* form | -*ta* form | -*ba* form |
|---|---|---|---|---|---|
| *shiraseru*<br>知らせる<br>tell, report | *shirasemasu*<br>知らせます | *shirasete*<br>知らせて | *shirasenai*<br>知らせない | *shiraseta*<br>知らせた | *shirasereba*<br>知らせれば |
| *sugiru*<br>過ぎる<br>pass, be over (i) | *sugimasu*<br>過ぎます | *sugite*<br>過ぎて | *suginai*<br>過ぎない | *sugita*<br>過ぎた | *sugireba*<br>過ぎれば |
| *suteru*<br>捨てる<br>throw away | *sutemasu*<br>捨てます | *sutete*<br>捨てて | *sutenai*<br>捨てない | *suteta*<br>捨てた | *sutereba*<br>捨てれば |
| *taberu*<br>食べる<br>eat | *tabemasu*<br>食べます | *tabete*<br>食べて | *tabenai*<br>食べない | *tabeta*<br>食べた | *tabereba*<br>食べれば |
| *tomeru*<br>止める<br>stop (t) | *tomemasu*<br>止めます | *tomete*<br>止めて | *tomenai*<br>止めない | *tometa*<br>止めた | *tomereba*<br>止めれば |
| *torikaeru*<br>取り替える<br>change, exchange | *torikaemasu*<br>取り替えます | *torikaete*<br>取り替えて | *torikaenai*<br>取り替えない | *torikaeta*<br>取り替えた | *torikaereba*<br>取り替えれば |
| *tsukareru*<br>疲れる<br>get tired | *tsukaremasu*<br>疲れます | *tsukarete*<br>疲れて | *tsukarenai*<br>疲れない | *tsukareta*<br>疲れた | *tsukarereba*<br>疲れれば |
| *tsukeru*<br>付ける<br>fix, attach, put together (t) | *tsukemasu*<br>付けます | *tsukete*<br>付けて | *tsukenai*<br>付けない | *tsuketa*<br>付けた | *tsukereba*<br>付ければ |
| *tsutomeru*<br>勤める<br>work for | *tsutomemasu*<br>勤めます | *tsutomete*<br>勤めて | *tsutomenai*<br>勤めない | *tsutometa*<br>勤めた | *tsutomereba*<br>勤めれば |
| *tsuzukeru*<br>続ける<br>continue (t) | *tsuzukemasu*<br>続けます | *tsuzukete*<br>続けて | *tsuzukenai*<br>続けない | *tsuzuketa*<br>続けた | *tsuzukereba*<br>続ければ |
| *wasureru*<br>忘れる<br>forget | *wasuremasu*<br>忘れます | *wasurete*<br>忘れて | *wasurenai*<br>忘れない | *wasureta*<br>忘れた | *wasurereba*<br>忘れれば |
| *yameru*<br>やめる<br>quit, stop | *yamemasu*<br>やめます | *yamete*<br>やめて | *yamenai*<br>やめない | *yameta*<br>やめた | *yamereba*<br>やめれば |

| conditional | potential | volitional | passive | causative |
|---|---|---|---|---|
| *shirasetara*<br>知らせたら | *shiraserareru*<br>知らせられる | *shiraseyō*<br>知らせよう | *shiraserareru*<br>知らせられる | *shirasesaseru*<br>知らせさせる |
| *sugitara*<br>過ぎたら | *sugirareru*<br>過ぎられる | *sugiyō*<br>過ぎよう | *sugirareru*<br>過ぎられる | *sugiraseru*<br>過ぎさせる |
| *sutetara*<br>捨てたら | *suterareru*<br>捨てられる | *suteyō*<br>捨てよう | *suterareru*<br>捨てられる | *sutesaseru*<br>捨てさせる |
| *tabetara*<br>食べたら | *taberareru*<br>食べられる | *tabeyō*<br>食べよう | *taberareru*<br>食べられる | *tabesaseru*<br>食べさせる |
| *tometara*<br>止めたら | *tomerareru*<br>止められる | *tomeyō*<br>止めよう | *tomerareru*<br>止められる | *tomesaseru*<br>止めさせる |
| *torikaetara*<br>取り替えたら | *torikaerareru*<br>取り替えられる | *torikaeyō*<br>取り替えよう | *torikaerareru*<br>取り替えられる | *torikaesaseru*<br>取り替えさせる |
| *tsukaretara*<br>疲れたら | *tsukarerareru*<br>疲れられる | *tsukareyō*<br>疲れよう | —<br>— | *tsukaresaseru*<br>疲れさせる |
| *tsuketara*<br>付けたら | *tsukerareru*<br>付けられる | *tsukeyō*<br>付けよう | *tsukerareru*<br>付けられる | *tsukesaseru*<br>付けさせる |
| *tsutometara*<br>勤めたら | *tsutomerareru*<br>勤められる | *tsutomeyō*<br>勤めよう | *tsutomerareru*<br>勤められる | *tsutomesaseru*<br>勤めさせる |
| *tsuzuketara*<br>続けたら | *tsuzukerareru*<br>続けられる | *tsuzukeyō*<br>続けよう | *tsuzukerareru*<br>続けられる | *tsuzukesaseru*<br>続けさせる |
| *wasuretara*<br>忘れたら | *wasurerareru*<br>忘れられる | *wasureyō*<br>忘れよう | *wasurerareru*<br>忘れられる | *wasuresaseru*<br>忘れさせる |
| *yametara*<br>やめたら | *yamerareru*<br>やめられる | *yameyō*<br>やめよう | *yamerareru*<br>やめられる | *yamesaseru*<br>やめさせる |

## Group 3

| plain form | -*masu* form | -*te* form | -*nai* form | -*ta* form | -*ba* form |
| --- | --- | --- | --- | --- | --- |
| *kuru*<br>来る<br>come | *kimasu*<br>来ます | *kite*<br>来て | *konai*<br>来ない | *kita*<br>来た | *kureba*<br>来れば |
| *suru*<br>する<br>do | *shimasu*<br>します | *shite*<br>して | *shinai*<br>しない | *shita*<br>した | *sureba*<br>すれば |

## Copula

| plain form | -*masu* form | -*te* form | -*nai* form | -*ta* form | -*ba* form |
| --- | --- | --- | --- | --- | --- |
| *da*<br>だ<br>be | *desu*<br>です | *de*<br>で | *de wa nai*<br>ではない | *datta*<br>だった | *de areba*<br>であれば |

| conditional | potential | volitional | passive | causative |
| --- | --- | --- | --- | --- |
| *kitara*<br>来たら | *korareru*<br>来られる | *koyō*<br>来よう | *korareru*<br>来られる | *kosaseru*<br>来させる |
| *shitara*<br>したら | *dekiru* ②<br>できる ② | *shiyō*<br>しよう | *sareru*<br>される | *saseru*<br>させる |

| conditional | potential | volitional | passive | causative |
| --- | --- | --- | --- | --- |
| *dattara*<br>だったら | — | *darō* (formal: *deshō*)<br>だろう (でしょう) | — | — |

# Index

The */-nai/* and */-masu/* stems, which are placed within slashes and struck-through in the body of the text, are here placed in brackets only since striking-through type this small would result in illegibility.

日本語の動詞
JAPANESE VERBS AT A GLANCE

1996年7月26日　第1刷発行

著　者　　茅野直子

発行者　　野間佐和子

発行所　　講談社インターナショナル株式会社
　　　　　〒112 東京都文京区音羽 1-17-14
　　　　　電話：03-3944-6493

印刷所　　株式会社　平河工業社

製本所　　株式会社　堅省堂

定価はカバーに表示してあります。
© 茅野直子　1996
Printed in Japan
ISBN4-7700-1985-8